FROM TECHIE TO BOSS

TRANSITIONING TO LEADERSHIP

Scott Cromar

From Techie to Boss: Transitioning to Leadership

ISBN-13 (pbk): 978-1-4302-5932-9

ISBN-13 (electronic): 978-1-4302-5933-6

Trademarked names, logos, and images may appear in this book. Rather than use a trademark symbol with every occurrence of a trademarked name, logo, or image we use the names, logos, and images only in an editorial fashion and to the benefit of the trademark owner, with no intention of infringement of the trademark.

The use in this publication of trade names, trademarks, service marks, and similar terms, even if they are not identified as such, is not to be taken as an expression of opinion as to whether or not they are subject to proprietary rights.

Portions of Chapter 9 are reproduced from Scott Cromar "Troubleshooting Methods" in *SysAdmin Magazine* (August 2007) and Scott Cromar *Solaris Troubleshooting Handbook* (2008) by permission.

While the advice and information in this book are believed to be true and accurate at the date of publication, neither the authors nor the editors nor the publisher can accept any legal responsibility for any errors or omissions that may be made. The publisher makes no warranty, express or implied, with respect to the material contained herein.

President and Publisher: Paul Manning
Acquisitions Editor: Robert Hutchinson
Editorial Board: Steve Anglin, Mark Beckner, Ewan Buckingham, Gary Cornell, Louise Corrigan, Morgan Ertel, Jonathan Gennick, Jonathan Hassell, Robert Hutchinson, Michelle Lowman, James Markham, Matthew Moodie, Jeff Olson, Jeffrey Pepper, Douglas Pundick, Ben Renow-Clarke, Dominic Shakeshaft, Gwenan Spearing, Matt Wade, Tom Welsh
Coordinating Editor: Rita Fernando
Copy Editor: Judy Ann Levine
Compositor: SPi Global
Indexer: SPi Global
Cover Designer: Anna Ishchenko

Distributed to the book trade worldwide by Springer Science+Business Media New York, 233 Spring Street, 6th Floor, New York, NY 10013. Phone 1-800-SPRINGER, fax (201) 348-4505, e-mail orders-ny@springer-sbm.com, or visit www.springeronline.com. Apress Media, LLC is a California LLC and the sole member (owner) is Springer Science + Business Media Finance Inc (SSBM Finance Inc). SSBM Finance Inc is a Delaware corporation.

For information on translations, please e-mail rights@apress.com, or visit www.apress.com.

Apress and friends of ED books may be purchased in bulk for academic, corporate, or promotional use. eBook versions and licenses are also available for most titles. For more information, reference our Special Bulk Sales–eBook Licensing web page at www.apress.com/bulk-sales.

Any source code or other supplementary materials referenced by the author in this text is available to readers at www.apress.com. For detailed information about how to locate your book's source code, go to www.apress.com/source-code/.

Apress Business: The Unbiased Source of Business Information

Apress business books provide essential information and practical advice, each written for practitioners by recognized experts. Busy managers and professionals in all areas of the business world—and at all levels of technical sophistication—look to our books for the actionable ideas and tools they need to solve problems, update and enhance their professional skills, make their work lives easier, and capitalize on opportunity.

Whatever the topic on the business spectrum—entrepreneurship, finance, sales, marketing, management, regulation, information technology, among others—Apress has been praised for providing the objective information and unbiased advice you need to excel in your daily work life. Our authors have no axes to grind; they understand they have one job only—to deliver up-to-date, accurate information simply, concisely, and with deep insight that addresses the real needs of our readers.

It is increasingly hard to find information—whether in the news media, on the Internet, and now all too often in books—that is even-handed and has your best interests at heart. We therefore hope that you enjoy this book, which has been carefully crafted to meet our standards of quality and unbiased coverage.

We are always interested in your feedback or ideas for new titles. Perhaps you'd even like to write a book yourself. Whatever the case, reach out to us at editorial@apress.com and an editor will respond swiftly. Incidentally, at the back of this book, you will find a list of useful related titles. Please visit us at www.apress.com to sign up for newsletters and discounts on future purchases.

The Apress Business Team

To Lisa,

the love of my life

Contents

About the Author

Scott Cromar is Senior Manager, Information Systems and Technology at Convergys. He was formerly a Vice President of Technology at the Bank of America/Merrill Lynch. He has been a Unix system administrator for two decades, and a project manager, technical team lead, and system architect for more than a decade, periodically building multifunctional operational teams from scratch. He earned his BS in mathematics from Brigham Young University and took an MSCIS in IT Project Management and Information Security from Boston University. Formerly administrator of the Solaris environment at Princeton University, Cromar is the author of *Solaris Troubleshooting Handbook* and numerous technical articles.

About the Contributor

David M. Jacobs is Director of Investment Administration Services Technology at Citigroup. He was formerly Manager of Application Development and Integration at Caxton Associates. He has been a software development manager and application programmer for more than three decades, building and integrating a variety of applications with globally dispersed teams. He earned his BA in mathematics and computer science from Queens College of the City University of New York.

Acknowledgments

Thank you to Lisa, Nicholas, and William. Without your support, this book would not have been possible.

Robert, Rita, and the rest of the Apress staff have made writing this book a wonderful experience. Thank you for your professionalism, encouragement, and support throughout the publication process.

Thank you to David for bringing your experience, professionalism and enthusiasm to the project. The book is much better thanks to your ideas, encouragement, and direct contributions.

Finally, thank you to my coworkers, bosses, and subordinates. Each of you has taught me something during my working career. I hope I have reflected the lessons you taught me fairly and accurately in this book.

Introduction

Let's face it: nontechnical managers just don't understand what we techies do for a living. The good ones try really hard and stand up for their team, but they just don't feel it in their bones. If technology is not stamped into your DNA, you just don't get it.

So that means that only technical people should manage technical people, right?

Here's the problem: technical people frequently do not make good managers. It isn't that we techies aren't smart enough—usually the best technicians are the people who are asked to step into leadership roles. But the skills that make a good techie are not necessarily the skills that make a good leader.

When you become a leader, the focus shifts. It is no longer about what you can accomplish as an individual contributor. You will be judged by your team's accomplishments.

Good technical people have developed good study habits, a sense of responsibility, and a solid work ethic. All of these are important and can translate into skills that will help you be a good leader. But you will only be an effective leader when you inspire your team members to reach their potential.

Moving into a leadership role can be a bumpy ride. But it can also be hugely rewarding. Make sure to approach it from the right frame of mind. It isn't about you anymore; it is about your team.

This book lays out some of the lessons I have learned during my own transition from a front-line techie to a manager.

Every environment is different, and every leader is coming from a slightly different place. I would love to hear your feedback about your own experiences, and how to make this book better. Please add your comments to my blog at http://fromtechietoboss.com.

You are embarking on an exciting new phase of your career and your life.

Good luck and God speed!

Moving into Management

You're respected by people inside and outside of your group. When there are hard problems to be resolved, you're the person who makes things work on time and under budget. More than once, you've pulled a complete miracle out of your hat. And when the team needs a new manager or team lead, you're the person at the top of the list.

Unfortunately, the skills that make a good technical staff member do not always translate well to management. How do you make the leap?

There are a lot of pitfalls for people making the leap from technician to manager or team lead. A typical scenario is the IT hero syndrome:

- You know that you can do things better, so you do them yourself.

- You get frustrated with your team members because they aren't pulling their weight.

- The situation deteriorates as you assign yourself more and more of the difficult work.

- You spend so much time solving technical problems, you fail to provide leadership to your team.

- You make yourself the indispensable person—right up until the moment you burn out.

It is one of the ironies of life that just as you really get good at a job, you are promoted to a new level of responsibility requiring skills that you may or may not have developed. Most companies do not have a new manager training program to teach you how to step up to the next level, and experienced managers may not remember how difficult it is to make the transition.

In this book I will share some of the tips and skills that I have learned the hard way, by transitioning from a solid performer to a team manager. There are a lot of resources available to help you make the transition.

Your entire world has changed. You are no longer judged by how elegantly you can resolve a technical puzzle. Now you are judged by how effectively your team can make the environment work to the benefit of the whole organization.

This book is all about proving that you are an exception to the Peter Principle.

Peter Principle   People in an organization tend to rise to their level of incompetence.

Right from the Start

Today's tech world is more fast-paced than at any other time in history. You should know; you have been part of what keeps that world humming. The rule of thumb is that you have 90 days to define how your term as a manager will evolve. During this time, you set a tone and communicate expectations to your team and to your superiors. You can fix mistakes later, but it is much harder, and there will be a tendency to backslide into the rut established in the first 90 days.

The first 90 days of your new job are a project. Approach this project with a plan. You don't have a plan if you just have a vague idea of how you want things to be. You have a plan when you have written down specific goals and timelines. Then you make yourself accountable for carrying out your plan by presenting it to your manager.

This is scary stuff, especially for a new manager.

Every team and every situation is different, but they tend to fall into a few larger categories:

- Your team is a successful team with a history and established procedures. Your role is envisioned as continuing the successful policies of the past. Any stumble or bobble will be viewed as a sign of weakness in the new manager.

- Your team has had problems in the past. There may be interpersonal tensions, and you may be replacing someone who was fired. Maybe the team is doing something well, but it is not aligned with the rest of the organization. Your role is to turn the team around, and the clock is ticking.

- Your team is new, either in a new organization or filling a new role in an existing organization. Your role may not be entirely defined, and there may not be any procedures in place for even the simplest functions. You'll have a brief honeymoon period, but then you will face divergent expectations by different stakeholders, who will want you to fix their most pressing problem. Now.

Teams all require similar things, but there is no way to put them all in place at the same time. You only have 24 hours in your day, and you should not use them all at work. You have to prioritize your goals. What does your team needs most?

Just to emphasize: you have to prioritize what your team needs. Not what you feel most comfortable with. Not your greatest technical strength. Not the most interesting technical project. What your team needs.

Characteristics of a Good Leader

There may be several of your team members who saw themselves in the team manager role. They may resent that you were given the job instead—regardless of whether you came from outside or were promoted from within.

The hard part is that you have to earn your team's respect. What makes this even harder is that this type of interpersonal dynamic does not come naturally to many skilled technical people.

There is no easy way to get peoples' respect. But there are some characteristics that go a long way toward earning it:

- **Be fair-minded.** Put yourself in the other person's shoes. Try to understand how things look from the other side of the fence. You don't have to give in to their demands, and you don't have to adopt their world view, just understand and respect it. This applies to your subordinates, your management, and your customers.

- **Be honest.** This includes telling people what you intend to do, setting reasonable expectations, and coming clean when you mess up or when you are not going to be able to deliver as promised.

- **Be ethical.** There will be many opportunities to take advantage of your employer or your subordinates. Don't. You have an internal compass; you know what is right and what is not. Do the right thing. Even if it makes people mad at you, they will respect you for sticking to your guns.

- **Be approachable.** Your subordinates and customers are going to see problems before you do. How are you going to find out about these problems if you don't make yourself available, physically and emotionally, for them to talk to you?

- **Have clear expectations.** Your team is made of professionals who want to make things work the right way. The manager's job is to provide a clear set of expectations that your technical staff can meet.

- **Recognize achievement.** How will your team understand what you want, if you don't point it out when they do it?

- **Identify and resolve failures.** Problems don't just disappear; they fester. Take them on, find a resolution, and fix them.

Being the boss is different from being a good team member. You are not just another teammate any more. It is your job to set the direction, strategy, and tone for the team. If you aren't willing to make the tough decisions, they aren't going to be made. If you don't keep your team's respect, they will fight against the decisions you have to make. But if you don't trust your team members, you will not inspire them to reach their potential.

GOOD LEADERSHIP IS ABOUT BALANCE

Set standards, but allow flexibility for team members to exercise their strengths.

Emphasize delegation and collaboration.

Be accessible, but maintain discipline.

Be decisive, but make the decisions after you understand the situation. Recognize that one of your team members may know more than you do—don't be afraid to ask questions.

Make the tough decisions, but be humane and fair. Leaders lead. They don't hide from responsibility.

Simplicity is almost always better than complexity.

Develop a healthy respect for Murphy's Law. If something can go wrong, have a way to recover from it.

Establish reliable, repeatable processes. Good processes help your team do jobs consistently and well. Then look for ways to improve those processes.

Challenge the status quo and look for ways to improve the environment.

Analysis Paralysis

Many decisions that you will face as a manager have to be made quickly, in the heat of the moment. You may not have all the information you want before you have to make a decision.

Weak leaders wait until they have every last bit of information before proceeding on anything. Unfortunately, by the time they have the information they need, the opportunity has passed by.

There will be times when you have to make a decision without having enough information. Here are some questions you can ask yourself to focus your thinking before making a decision.

Is there more relevant information that can be obtained quickly? You will never have all the information, and you will only rarely have the optimal amount of information to make the best possible decision.

What are the downside risks of the different options? If the risks are too great, you may need to decide to delay your final decision. (Just remember that deciding to delay is itself a decision that has its own set of downside risks.)

What is driving a quicker decision? Are there real priorities being expressed or just a preference for action?

When you do make a decision, own it. Part of being a leader is accepting the consequences of your decisions.

After the decision is made and the impact of your decision is known, circle back to look at the decision itself and the process used to make it. Were there better options? What additional information would you have needed to choose the other option? Are there ways to make adjustments to improve the situation? Are there ways that you can start gathering information now to make other, similar decisions better in the future?

Modeling Behavior

Good leaders model the behavior they request from their team members. For example, if you ask for punctuality, be punctual. If you ask team members to deliver their commitments on time, deliver your commitments to them on time. If you ask for responsiveness, be responsive.

One of the quickest ways to lose your team's respect is to be seen as a hypocrite. You are asking your team to work hard; work at least as hard. You are asking them to think outside the box; be innovative in helping your team accomplish its tasks.

You are a member of your team. Granted, you have a unique role within the team. But your team members will expect you to live up to the expectations that you set for other team members.

Messaging

We technical people like to make fun of marketers. Dilbert creator Scott Adams has made a mint from comic strips showing marketers in a bad light. But they may have something to teach us.

Identify the characteristics you want your team to embody. Then market your team in terms of those characteristics. Message relentlessly.

Messaging is different from nagging. Don't walk around pointing at everything that is not the way you want it to be. Instead, recognize excellence. Send team emails congratulating a team member for exemplifying one or another characteristic that you consider important (and cc your boss on those emails). Catch people doing the right thing, and thank them for it. Write things on white boards. Put up posters. When you talk about your team, describe your team as you want it to be.

Above all, never give up. Continue to message about your team every chance you get. If people make fun of you for it, laugh along with them because sometimes it does seem a little silly. Then get right back to it.

But the most effective messaging is the message you send by your own example. When you define a characteristic as being important, your personal behavior should be a sterling example of that characteristic.

The Principle of Leverage

The key to effective management is leverage. You are only one person. To succeed and accomplish anything really great, you need to motivate and train your team to accomplish far more than you can achieve by yourself.

For a lot of technical managers, this is a hard thing to learn. After all, you may have been put into the leadership position precisely because you are more adept technically than the rest of the team. The challenge is to bring the team up to your standard.

Think of yourself as a seed crystal. Team members will gravitate to structure. Provide a reasonable way for the rest of the team to fit as part of a durable whole. This will involve mentoring, training, and a heck of a lot more time and effort than it would take for you to just do the job yourself. But that's what it means to be a leader, not just a really good tech.

This does not mean that you should become a micromanager. In fact, you have to avoid becoming a micromanager. Follow up with your direct reports to check on their progress. Make sure they are not facing obstacles they can't overcome. But don't hover. If your team members don't have the space to try things out and even make mistakes, they will not grow. If they don't grow, that means that you fail.

It can be even harder to make this transition if you have to fill both your old and new positions at the same time. This is not uncommon, especially if you are promoted from within and have to backfill your old position. Separate the thought patterns you need to carry out your old responsibilities from those you need for your new position. Work to transition out of your old responsibilities as well as you can, as quickly as you can.

Transparency

One of the toughest parts of leading a team is getting everyone marching in the same direction. You can try to just give orders. Good luck with that. To really be effective, you need to get your team members to buy into what you are trying to accomplish. When you can get your team members using their individual skills to accomplish a single goal, you have become a good leader.

For you to get your team moving in the right direction, you have to develop a habit of transparency. Without transparency, your team will not have a good understanding of why they are doing what they are doing, and what the priorities are. If they do not understand their role in the overall scheme of things, they will be forced to wait for you to tell them what to do next. This is not where you need to be.

In a transparent environment, solutions to difficult problems may come from people who have different points of view and different skill sets. A good solution is much more likely to emerge in a collaborative environment. If the manager is the only one proposing ideas, the team is in serious trouble.

When the entire team is involved in the planning process, they become invested in the project. The team members understand the reasons for the different steps in the plan, and they will have a better idea how to react to unexpected issues that may arise.

Micromanaging is horribly inefficient. When a manager relies on micromanaging rather than transparency, team members will frequently freeze in place waiting for instructions before proceeding. In a team where transparency has become a habit, people will be able to think and reason for themselves, and will be able to select an appropriate course of action.

Your team needs to be productive. It can't be fully productive unless they understand what they are doing and have the freedom to execute the task appropriately.

Effective managers operate in a different space than team members do. Team members typically need to focus on the details of a finite number of discrete tasks, while a leader needs to understand the shape of the overall problem.

The key is to communicate the scope of the problem and the approach to solving the problem so that the individual contributors can tie their efforts together.

Enabling Your Team Members

One of the most useful things you can do as a manager is to clear roadblocks out of your team's way. Find out what is keeping your team members from doing a better job, and help them fix it.

Help team members communicate tricks and tips among themselves. Recognize team members who enable their teammates to do a better job. Ask your team members to provide their best work, and recognize them when they do.

Problems Caused by Poor Leadership

A team is more than a group of talented people. A team is formed to work together to accomplish a goal. If the talented individuals do not have clear direction, each will make decisions based on what that particular person knows.

When a team has a weak leader, everyone only understands a small piece of the overall project or environment.

Here are some common reactions to weak leadership:

- **Inaction.** Someone may be afraid of doing the wrong thing, and do nothing at all while waiting for instructions. Progress grinds to a halt.

- **Individual judgment.** Someone may proceed based on an understanding of a small piece of the puzzle and cause problems elsewhere in the project.

- **Conflicting priorities.** Team members may work on tasks in an order that does not match the organization's needs; this results in project delays or an unstable environment.

The leader's responsibility is to help the team members to see how their particular part fits into the overall whole. A good leader helps his team understand the end goal, how every contribution is important to achieving the goal, and why the goal is important.

In short, a good leader inspires and organizes the team to work together to help the organization meet its overall goals.

The Core Challenges

You don't have a lot of time to make the necessary changes. In most environments, you may have 90 days to get your team working toward a common plan and achieving real results. If you haven't made measurable progress toward your end goals by then, you are in trouble.

Management guru Michael Watkins categorizes the key challenges facing a new manager as being the following.[1]

- **Promote yourself.** Your company has promoted you. Now you need to promote yourself. Break away from your old thought patterns. Make the transition to thinking like a manager. If you don't do this in the beginning of your tenure, it will be increasingly difficult to do it later on.

- **Learn fast and well.** Learn as much as possible about the organization as quickly as possible. This includes information about what the company does, and how the company does it. It also includes information about the company culture, and how it affects the overall company mission.

- **Identify the right strategy.** Every job is different. Don't stick slavishly to a plan, even one that worked somewhere else. Come up with a plan that will work here and now. If your initial plan is not going to work, change it so that the new plan has a ghost of a chance of working.

- **Achieve early wins.** Early wins build team momentum and credibility. You will need both to tackle your team's challenges going forward.

- **Negotiate success.** Manage your boss's expectations. Present a 90-day plan to your boss, identify the early wins you expect to accomplish, and negotiate what success will mean for those early wins.

---

[1]Michael Watkins, *The First 90 Days* (Boston, MA: Harvard Business School Press, 2003).

- **Align.** Work with your boss, your peers, and your partners to make sure that your team is pulling in a direction that helps the overall company mission.

- **Build your team.** Evaluate your team's members. You have to pick the right structure for your team. And you have to select the right people for the right slots.

- **Create coalitions.** Just as your team needs to work together to really get things done, your team needs to fit into the larger landscape for the company to move forward. Identify people whose support you need, and figure out how to work together with them.

- **Keep your balance.** There is a lot to do, more than you actually can do. Prioritize. Keep your sense of perspective. And remember what your overall goals are.

- **Transition others.** The faster you can get your direct reports, your bosses, and your partners used to how things work now, the faster you can start to achieve the results you were hired to achieve.

We discussed the challenge of promoting yourself in the previous section. Keep the other challenges in mind while reading the rest of the book, especially when working on your 90-day plan.

Avoid mistakes by engaging your team and listening to them. Instill a sense of discipline about verifying and validating. Have the right information before you make a decision.

CONSEQUENCES OF POOR MANAGEMENT

Kenneth Brill of the Uptime Institute[2] reports that only a third of data center failures are caused by equipment failures. Of the remainder, 70% are caused by management decisions or management inaction.

When you are a team member, you may cause problems by making a mistake. When you are in charge of the environment, the types of mistakes you can make are magnified. That is why most serious problems are ultimately caused by management decisions.

[2] Kenneth G. Brill, "It's Management's Fault," *Forbes*, July 1, 2009.

Summary

Technical managers seem to have a harder time transitioning to leadership than most other people. Part of this is that technical excellence comes from intense study, frequently alone. Part is that technical managers are frequently selected for their technical skills, not their leadership experience. But technical people are smart and motivated. With help and guidance, technical people can become some of your strongest leaders.

Discussion Questions

1.   Who was a manager that you particularly admired? What did that manager do to earn your respect?

2.   Put yourself in your new manager's shoes. What are the biggest challenges on your manager's plate?

3.   What opportunities do you see for improvement in your environment? Which of them can your team achieve in 30 days?

4.   What are the biggest challenges your subordinates face? How can you help them succeed?

Further Reading

Berkun, Scott. *Making Things Happen*. Sebastopol, CA: O'Reilly, 2008.

Brill, Kenneth G. "It's Management's Fault," *Forbes*, July 1, 2009. Available at: www.forbes.com/2009/07/01/management-catastrophic-failure-technology-cio-network-management.html.

Harvard Business Essentials. *Manager's Toolkit*. Boston, MA: Harvard Business School Press, 2004.

Watkins, Michael. *The First 90 Days*. Boston, MA: Harvard Business School Press, 2003.

Your Transition Plan

Congratulations! You're in charge. Or are you?

When you start a new leadership position, you do not have the luxury of a settling-in period. Given the pace of the modern IT environment, pausing to catch your breath would be a deadly mistake.

At the same time, you can't do everything all at once. Your team may not know you, or at least does not know you as a leader. The team is not yet the well-oiled execution machine that you will build later. The team is still a bunch of people trying to figure out who the new boss is, and what the boss wants. Depending on the history of the group, some of your team members may not have your best interest or even the best interest of the company at heart. You have to lay the groundwork to get the team moving in the right direction.

Start by focusing on a few early wins. This will teach the team how you like to operate, get them used to achieving within that framework, and buy you some breathing room from your own boss.

Identifying early wins depends on what you learn about the environment, what your boss expects of you, and the direction you want to take the team. Select early win tasks that address all three issues. This is not the time to pick a fight.

A change in leadership is a tremendous opportunity for the organization to make needed changes in direction.

But it is also a time when the incoming leader is vulnerable. The new boss has not had time to develop the working relationships or loyalty needed to make the team work effectively.

Be aware of the vulnerability, but don't be captured by it. Embrace the opportunity.

Team Building

In your first 90 days, you have to build your team, and learn to make your team work well within the overall organization.

One of the most critical drivers to your team's success will lie in the decisions you make about how to structure your team. You have to decide on an appropriate structure for the team, and who will fill which roles within it. The earlier you make these decisions, the more you will be able to leverage the changes during your first critical 90 days.

The irony is that you may need to make these decisions after insufficient time to learn about the people in your team, and what their strengths and weaknesses are.

So you will have to gather as much high-quality information as you can, as quickly as you can. Interview team members personally. Speak with key stakeholders in other groups to get insight. But don't get caught up in the echo chamber of the first person to catch your ear. Sometimes the most insight is held by the members of the team who are least likely to speak up. You have to gather the information quickly, but also filter the bad information from the good.

Besides building your team from within, you also need to be building relationships with other supporting teams. Your team needs to fit into the landscape of the overall organization.

Some of the people you are supervising may be jealous of your new position, especially if you are promoted to supervise people who were once your peers. Expect that your leadership will be challenged. Meet those challenges with firmness, fairness, and decency. If some people in your organization simply will not accept you as the leader, they will need to be moved out of your organization, the sooner the better.

The way you meet these challenges will set the tone for your tenure as the leader of the team. Grasp each challenge as an opportunity to set the tone for your team as it will become.

Evaluate Your Team

If you have inherited an existing team, you need to speak with them as early as you can. You need to find out who does what, how each person works, and who is ready to follow directions.

You also need to find out who is willing to give you a chance. Some team members may not be happy about you as their new manager. Try to work it out, but be prepared to shift them out of your team if necessary.

Don't let problems fester. There is a temptation to ignore problems, but they will get worse rather than better. Try to address issues head-on, usually in one-on-one discussions. Explain your expectations and ask for a commitment. Make it clear that comments are welcome, and plans may be adjusted as the situation evolves, but the plan is the plan. The manager's job is to define the plan; the team member's job is to execute it.

Read the evaluations left by your predecessor, but take them with a grain of salt. Not all managers are entirely objective, and you need to be wary of evidence that the previous manager may have played favorites at evaluation time.

Take a look at the group dynamics to see how team members work together. Identify which strengths and weaknesses exist in the communication and interaction between team members.

You will need to identify which team members fall into which of the following categories:

- **Key player.** Keep these people where they are.

- **Development project.** This person isn't quite there, but shows potential. Work out a plan to develop it.

- **Move.** This person might fit better in a different role.

- **Observe.** You aren't going to figure out everyone right away. Give yourself space to watch and think if you aren't sure.

- **Replace eventually.** This person should be replaced, but it can be done at the right time.

- **Replace immediately.** Find a way to move this person out. This can either be someone who has an attitude problem that can't be resolved, or someone who is irredeemably incompetent.

Early Wins

The type of task that you select for an early win depends on the type of environment you have inherited. The strategy you employ needs to match the situation you find yourself in.

Even the definition of a "win" can shift over time. When you make your 90-day plan, present it to your boss. Get buy-in and define what success means, and how it will be measured.

Your boss, your peers, and your partners can also help align your priorities with the organization's priorities. If you are succeeding at something that is less important to the overall organization, you are failing to reach your potential.

Organizational Wins

Some of your early wins may be organizational. Not all of these may be reportable to your boss, but you need to accomplish them to get your team off to a good start. Track these on your 90-day plan, and don't let yourself get sidetracked from taking care of them:

- **Get to know your team.** Talk to each of them. Find out who they are, what they like to do, and what they want to do.

- **Get acquainted with your colleagues.** Find out how they work, and what their expectations are of your team.

- **Talk to your boss.** Find out what your boss's expectations are.

- **Find out how your team is currently structured.** Who does what? Who owns what?

If you haven't gathered this information, it will be impossible for you to work on your first early win: Structure the team for success.

Structure the Team for Success

It may be the case that the team is already well structured. In that case, reinforce the parts of the structure that work. Assure the leaders that you like the work they have been doing, and encourage the staff members to continue.

It is more likely that there are some adjustments that need to be made. There may be someone on the team who is hoarding knowledge or interesting work. There may be someone who is more interested in exercising authority than performing with excellence. Or there may be someone on the team with potential that has not been realized yet.

As an outsider, you have an advantage. People within a team see the work that they have always done, divided up the way they have always divided it. Based on your conversations with your peers and your boss, you have a view into the work that needs to be done, and what the priorities are.

When you restructure the team, you do not have to divide up the same work the same way and just reshuffle the names. You can take what you know about what needs to be done, add some tasks, de-emphasize some other tasks, and divide up the work in a way that matches up with the people best able to execute it.

Spread learning experiences and interesting work around as far as possible. Design and evaluation tasks should be spread among several people, not just always assigned to the same person. Teach your team to work together on these plum tasks, and those same work habits will carry over to the less fun work.

You will probably make some mistakes, so make it clear that responsibilities will rotate over time, as appropriate. Set an expectation that things are not set in stone.

Also make it clear that you expect success as a team, and that you value and reward teamwork. Just as your power comes from leveraging your team, your employees' power comes from being part of a well-functioning team.

Defect Rates and Tracking Success

It is easy to claim early wins. Lots of people skate through their careers, claiming successes that they have not earned. You should be different: document your progress and track your successes.

Documenting and tracking progress needs to become second nature to your team. Set up a method for people to identify the work they are doing and to measure their success.

If you have a ticketing system, that is a good place to start. Work should be reflected on tickets, and the success of that work should be reported there. If you don't have a ticketing or work tracking system, implement one. That can be one of your early wins.

Whatever your team does, the key thing to measure is the defect rate. Defects are what trigger rework. Defects are counted differently for different disciplines, and you will need to define defects in a way that works for your team.

If you are gathering requirements, a defect would be having to circle back and redefine the requirement. If you are coding, a defect would be a *bug* (i.e., a failure to meet a requirement). If you are building a server, a defect would be having to go back and reconfigure something on the server.

What you want to see is the defect rate dropping over time. That doesn't happen by itself. The way to lower the defect rate is to analyze the defects and implement processes and procedures to avoid them. A better template for collecting requirements, a different type of code review process, or a more defined building process would be ways to correct the three types of defects we discussed earlier.

So, how do you track the defect rate?

It would be really cool if your team just collected and reported the defect rate, but that seems unlikely. Once you can convince your team of the power of tracking defects, you might be able to get them to do that.

Postmortems—On a Small Scale

One way of getting the team into the habit of tracking defects is to select work items (e.g., tickets) and ask your team members detailed questions about them. What were the time-intensive parts of that task? Which parts were frustrating? What mistakes were made? What rework was needed? How could the process have been changed to avoid those problems in the future? This sort of questioning is sometimes called a *postmortem*.

This is a habit your team should get into, and one that they should be able to execute without you. But you may need to jumpstart the habit by interviewing your team members individually or in groups about what they are working on. Take the time to listen and ask questions. You have an advantage that most managers don't—you know the technology, or at least you know technology well enough to ask penetrating questions.

Take notes about the defects in the process and the suggestions that are raised to help avoid them in the future. Circulate the suggestions in the group, and get suggestions from other group members. Foster the conversation, and then stand back and let it happen. Assign someone to rank the suggestions, and assign the best ones to team members for implementation.

This is not magic. Postmortems are a common enough discipline, in the context of major undertakings. But if you look at your team's work, most of it is done on a much smaller scale. Postmortems on a selected sample of common work items can result in a large overall improvement in your team's efficiency, and in your team's morale. Nobody likes rework.

How do you track the defect rate over time? There are a couple of ways to approach it. If you can get to where defects are self-reported consistently, you can track the defect rate directly. You can also sample a certain number of tickets of a certain type each month and look at them for defects, then track the defect rate and report it. Try to focus on work that is common and visible first. Those are the low-hanging fruit where your efforts will be most visible and have the best feedback effect by reducing the amount of time and effort your team spends executing them.

Once your team sees the power of postmortems, you will start to see team members executing them on their own. When you see that happening, you know that you have accomplished something.

Communication Structure

Leveraging your team will not be possible without communication. Your team should become used to communicating in a few standard ways. There is a balance between execution and communication. If people spend all their time on inefficient communication, they will have less time for executing the work.

It is most effective to standardize on a few ways of communicating. These should have different purposes and should be used appropriately.

- **Face-to-face.** In-person communication allows for faster transmission of information than other communications methods. Eighty percent of what is communicated face-to-face is nonverbal. Video conferencing can capture some of this nonverbal communication, and may be a reasonable alternative when travel is not practical.

- **Voice.** Telephone and conference calls allow for some of the nonverbal communication to take place. Tone and pacing can communicate as much as the actual words.

- **IM.** Most companies specify an instant messaging standard. The advantage over email is immediacy because most people respond to IM more rapidly than email. On the other hand, that means people can spend all their time messaging rather than working. Mentor your team members on when to use IM to best effect.

- **SMS.** This is similar instant messaging, but sent to a cell phone. I ask my team members to send me an SMS to notify me of an outage, or of a personal illness or emergency. That way, they can be reasonably sure that I will see their message right away.

- **Tickets.** Ticketing systems can allow for work to be submitted, then executed by the next available team member. All work requests should be submitted by ticket, not email. With tickets, team members can see if someone else has picked up the ticket, and the requestor can track progress as long as the implementer updates the ticket.

- **Calendaring.** I ask my team members to send their vacation and sick day requests by requesting a meeting on the calendar system. That way they have a way to track my approval, and I have a reminder of who is going to be out on which day. (This is in addition to the SMS to notify me if the person needs to take a sick day.)

From the beginning, set up expectations about how people should communicate. The expectations you set in the beginning will set the tone for the time you manage the group.

Challenging Environments

When senior executives were asked about the most influential positions they held in their careers, they typically pointed at positions that had involved major challenges.[1] These included turnarounds, positions with significant new responsibilities, start-ups, or relocations overseas. The fact is that we learn more from challenging assignments than easy ones. If you are coming into a challenging position, all the more reason to treat the transition seriously.

For a lot of technical managers, we tend to be stronger at technical challenges than at political or cultural challenges. Our impulse may be to focus on what we are strongest at, and ignore challenges in the other domains. It is counterproductive to ignore these challenges. There are some strategies for dealing with challenges that make us uncomfortable:

- **Self-discipline.** You have gotten as far as you have because you are able to focus on unpleasant tasks. Recognize that political and cultural challenges are part of your job, develop a plan to take care of them, and devote the time to execute your plan.

- **Find mentors.** You have developed relationships during your career. Many of those people can give you good advice about how to deal with the challenges that may not be up your alley, whether they are technical, political,

[1] Helen Handfield-Jones, "How Executives Grow," *McKinsey Quarterly*, February 2000.

or cultural. But deal with these people from the mindset of your new position, not your old one. You will not succeed unless your mentors and friends see you in the light of your new position.

- **Build your team.** Some members of your team may be able to help you with areas that are not a particular strength of yours. Ask them to assist you with these challenges, as opposed to avoiding challenges you would rather not face. Recognize that this is a skill you must develop to succeed.

Manage Expectations

You face expectations from several stakeholders. Your boss, your direct reports, and your internal customers all have needs and expectations. Your former boss may not be willing to let you go.

All of these expectations have to be managed, or they will eat you alive. If your former boss needs you to transition, set explicit expectations and deadlines. Your priority is your new job, not your old one.

With your new boss, sit down to develop a 90-day plan of action. Identify some specific milestones that your team will meet within that time frame, and specify what qualifies as success for each one.

Be aware that some people may not have your best interests at heart. People may be jealous, or may be looking to dump responsibilities that they don't want to carry any more. Some may be looking for a fall guy for a long-festering wound.

Keep an eye out, and concentrate on the areas that you have actually been assigned. Make sure that expectations are documented and clear. And then keep your boss up to date about progress on those tasks as well as any challenges you are working through.

And when you set expectations, always err on the side of under promising and over delivering. Allow yourself a margin of error, whether it be in terms of money or time. Something will always go wrong, so you need to allow for that in your plans.

Managing Your Boss

Part of managing is managing up, not just down. You have to develop a good working relationship with your boss. Your boss is ultimately the person who will give you the resources to succeed. Fighting with your boss is almost never a good idea.

There are some key pitfalls to keep in mind as your relationship with your boss develops:

- **Stay in touch.** You are responsible for keeping your boss up to date, not the other way around. Schedule regular one-on-one communication with your boss; otherwise other people in the organization will do your communicating for you. And you will almost certainly not like the results.

- **Come clean on problems.** Nobody likes to be the bearer of bad news. But it is all going to come out anyway, so it is better to communicate early rather than late. When you tell your boss about a problem, also explain what you are doing about it, and how and when you expect the problem to be resolved. If you handle this right, you can turn the problem resolution into one of your early wins.

- **Don't lecture the boss.** Your boss probably has a different working style from yours. You need to respect the difference and learn to work with it. This doesn't mean that you should try to mimic your boss's style; you need to develop your own style. But learn your boss's rhythms and how and when to communicate information and plans to fit into that style.

- **The relationship is your responsibility.** Don't expect your boss to make contact with you or ask you leading questions. You need to provide your boss with the information before your boss even knows that he or she needs it.

- **Negotiate expectations and timelines.** Part of providing the information is providing updates and renegotiating expectations if necessary. It is obviously better to negotiate solid timelines and expectations up front, if at all possible.

- **Align with the boss's priorities.** Just like you expect your direct reports to follow through on the tasks you assign them, your boss expects you to work on issues according to the priorities you are given.

- **Be aware of your boss's peer relationships.** Your boss gets information about your team from several sources. Be aware of who else is feeding your boss information, and make sure that they know what you are doing to help them with their priorities. If your boss is getting mixed messages about you, it will only undercut your effectiveness.

- **Don't touch the untouchables.** There may be particular areas where your boss does not want you interfering. It is important to identify those as early as possible, because it will be a waste of time and effort to take those on. You may have to rely on subtle cues like body language or the tone of a response to a query.

"Managing up" is one of the critical skills you will have to learn as a new manager. Observe how other managers interact with their manager. Tap into your network of mentors and friends for advice. Do whatever it takes to get this relationship right, or nothing else is going to work.

Drinking from the Fire Hose

Every new job brings new challenges, but new management jobs more than most. Not only do you have to learn a vast amount of information in a short amount of time; you are the one responsible for identifying and prioritizing what you need to learn so that you learn the most important things first.

Identify the most critical pieces of information you need, and then develop a plan for finding and verifying that information. If you just try to drink from the fire hose without structuring your learning efforts, you are not going to learn what you need to know in time to be able to use the information.

One key question that has to be answered is how things got to be the way they are. If you don't learn the history of the group, you are likely to make the same mistakes that were already made. The people who work for you are not stupid; they have probably tried a lot of different things. Maybe some of the things that look strange at first glance are just creative ways to work around an issue you may not realize that you have yet.

Admitting that you have to learn new information can be difficult. For some technical people, it can feel like an admission of weakness to admit that we don't know everything yet.

But we have to deal with reality as it exists. And reality is that we don't know everything, and we have a lot to learn in a short amount of time. Pride is just going to get in the way.

On top of that, the denial that comes with pride can cause us to start to blame our team members for our own failings. Once that dynamic gets started, nothing good will come of it.

Accept that you have a lot to learn. You are going to have to ask for help. It is not weakness; it is reality. Prioritize what you need to learn, make a plan, and get on with it.

What You Need to Find Out

There are several types of questions you need answered. Michael Watkins suggests several topics that you should explore when generating your list.[2] Here are some of the questions I ask; you will need to create a list for your environment.

- How have objectives been set for this team in the past?

- How well has this team met them?

- Do people external to the team agree with that assessment?

- Were the objectives appropriate? (Were the objectives too easy, or too hard?)

- How was success measured?

- What behaviors were encouraged by these measurements?

- Which behaviors were discouraged?

- What were the consequences if deliverables were late or of poor quality?

- What are the root causes of this team's successes?

- What else contributed to those successes?

- What caused or contributed to the team's failures?

- How has the environment (strategy, structure, team capabilities, culture, and politics) contributed to the team's success or failure? What changes have been attempted to the environment? What was the effect?

- Who has driven the changes that were attempted?

- What changes have been suggested but not attempted? Why?

- Is the stated strategy taking the organization in the right direction? Is it getting in the way? Or is it unclear?

---

[2]Michael Watkins, *The First 90 Days* (Boston, MA: Harvard Business School Press, 2003).

- Which team members have contributed to the successes and failures of the organization?

- Can less capable team members be trained to fill bigger roles or to behave in ways that contribute to success?

- Who can be trusted?

- Who has influence within the organization?

- How are the existing processes contributing to team success or failure?

- Are there hidden surprises in your team's environment that need to be addressed before they blow up?

- Are there cultural or political land mines that need to be avoided?

- What challenges does the organization face in the near term?

- What long-term challenges does the organization face?

- Are there opportunities that need to be exploited?

- What barriers have prevented change?

- Which teams are already performing at a high level?

- Which capabilities do we need to develop?

- Which aspects of our culture helped us to succeed or caused us to fail?

- Who has the authority to make decisions? Is that a function of the person's position, expertise, or personality?

- What actions within the organization are perceived as creating value? Which are perceived as destroying it?

- What structural or geographic culture differences exist within the organization?

- How do different professional groups (managers, engineers, and support staff) interact with each other?

- Where are policies and procedures documented? How complete is that repository? Are staff members following standard procedures where possible?

These are the questions you need to answer for yourself. You can't reasonably put these questions to everyone in the environment. But you can schedule the time to speak to individuals and ask them open-ended questions to get the information you need.

One problem to avoid is a bias toward the responses of the first people you interview. One technique for avoiding this problem is to start with the same script for everyone you interview. For example, the answers to the following open-ended questions will get you a lot of the information you need. They will need to be customized for your environment:

What challenges do you see, either now or in the near future?

Where are these challenges coming from? Are the causes internal or external?

What opportunities do you see that are not being exploited? What barriers are preventing them from being exploited? What do you see as the most important thing for me to focus on?

Keep notes, use the same script, and look for similarities and differences between the responses. This technique can be used (with different scripts, of course) to look at responses from your customers and peers as well as your team members. Compare responses from people at the same level as well as looking at responses within the same vertical within the organization.

Some information may also be available from things such as employee or customer satisfaction surveys. If it is not, find a way to take the temperature of both your team and its customer base.

If a root cause analysis has been run on areas where the team has failed, you will also need that information. If it has not, you may need to convene a group to investigate the failure and suggest responses. In Chapter 9, we discuss techniques to run a group troubleshooting session.

Conversations with Your Boss

One of your key constituents is your boss. You have to find out how your boss sees the situation to identify the early wins, align with the overall organization, and negotiate expectations.

Some key information that you need from your boss:

- **Current situation.** What are the characteristics of the environment as it exists today? Are you building it, are you continuing the success of a previous leader, or are major changes needed? You may not end up agreeing with your boss's diagnosis of the situation, but you will need to discuss that from a starting point of what the boss thinks today.

- **Expectations.** How will your performance be measured? What specific milestones do you need to hit?

- **Style.** How does your boss prefer to communicate? How should you present information? What level of information does your boss want you to provide, and how frequently?

- **Resources.** What do you need? How will you use it? When will the resources be needed? What is the impact of not getting some of the resources? (You may want to phrase this conversation in menu fashion, e.g.—"If you want x%, it will cost $y; a% will cost $b.")

- **Personal development.** How will your performance affect your growth within the organization? What is it you want, and how can your boss help you get it?

Not all of these questions should be addressed the first day. In fact, some of them require that you gather information beforehand or at least develop a level of trust between you and the boss.

In particular, the personal development conversation will need to wait until you have developed some trust with your boss, and hopefully after you have achieved some of your early wins.

These conversations will go better if you prepare beforehand. Your boss also needs to prepare, so agree to an agenda beforehand.

Draft a Learning Plan

At different stages in your 90-day plan, you need to include activities to learn the environment so that you can steer your team in the right direction. Include your learning plan in your overall 90-day plan. Here are some suggestions of the types of learning activities you can include for different stages of the 90-day plan.

Before Your First Day

Read external comments and articles by people who know your organization. Google is your friend. Look at write-ups in the annual report as well as news items and blog postings.

Speak with your group's suppliers or customers, if possible. Draft a script and look for commonalities and differences across these interviews.

If possible, speak with your predecessor. Depending on the situation, this may or may not be possible. Listen without being captured by the previous leader's world view. You will bring your own perspectives and talents into the environment, so you may or may not end up agreeing with what the former leader has to say.

Speak with your new boss. Try to understand both the environment as well as the boss's expectations for your team.

Generate hypotheses (discussed in Chapter 9). Then identify ways that you can confirm or refute these hypotheses. These should make their way into the next phase of your 90-day plan.

First Week

Review detailed internal information that was not available to you before starting. This may include items such as satisfaction surveys, the files of the people who work for you, and root cause analyses of problems.

Meet with each of your direct reports individually, and ask the questions from the script you developed in the last phase. Compare and contrast the responses, and use the information to adjust your hypotheses, and to develop the next round of scripts.

Talk to sales, customer service, and purchasing to see how they perceive your group. See if they can help you identify problems or opportunities to be exploited in your 90-day plan.

Ask people at different levels within the organization about the vision and strategy of the organization. Are the responses similar, or at least consistent? If your team is going to be successful, you need to be pulling in the same direction as the overall strategy, and the teams around you also need to be aligned.

Test your hypotheses about challenges and opportunities by checking first with lower-level people, and then use the same script at progressively higher levels within the organization. This will give you a feeling for how well information is filtering up.

At the end of your first week, discuss what you have found with your boss. Present your current hypotheses about challenges and opportunities, as well as your adjusted plan for the next phase.

First Month

Continue to follow up to confirm or refute the hypotheses you have developed. This will mean circling back to some of the people you have already spoken with, and it will mean requesting data to confirm or refute what you suspect is the situation.

Look at how people on the outside of your organization perceive you. When you ask questions to gather this information, start from the outside in. This will include people such as sales reps who are completely outside of the company, as well as your team's internal customers.

Examine some of the key processes that your team is responsible for. How are requests received, how are requirements specified and determined, and how are requests executed? Look for process improvements that will benefit both your customers and your team. Process improvements are usually fertile ground for early wins. Document these early wins for your boss; these will help you lock in the credibility you will need for harder changes you will need to make.

Find the old-timers and integrators within the organization. From them, you can learn organization history and why things are done the way they are. Maybe the processes are outmoded, but maybe there is a real reason for the way things are.

As you gather this information, update your hypotheses and your 90-day plan. Your 90-day plan cannot be viewed as a static document. Don't let yourself get locked in to your original hypotheses.

When you meet with your boss, present the changes you have made to your plan and explain why you made them. By this point, you should have identified some early wins, and hopefully even implemented some of them. Highlight these, and negotiate with your boss to identify the success criteria for each of these wins.

Second Month

The second month needs to be where you start putting some of your changes into place, and measuring the results. Ideally, you should have some early wins during the second month.

This is where metrics come into play. If you can't measure and list your accomplishments, everyone will assume you are just mouthing words. For each of the changes you are putting into place, identify a way to verify and measure the effect of the changes.

Third Month

At the 60-day mark, review your progress toward the overall 90-day plan, and make adjustments for the coming 30 days.

Don't be too proud to change the parts of your plan that aren't working the way you expected. Plans need to evolve to reflect the changing face of reality.

Matching the Strategy to the Situation

Broadly speaking, Michael Watkins identifies four major types of situations you may encounter as a new leader.[3]

1. **Start-up.** You are building a new team, possibly entirely from scratch.

2. **Turnaround.** The team or organization is in serious trouble that must be fixed now.

3. **Realignment.** Move a once successful team into sync with the larger organizations goals and requirements.

4. **Sustaining success.** Take over the leadership of an already successful organization.

Each of these situations has unique characteristics. For example, start-ups and turnarounds require that the leader make difficult and critical decisions right away, possibly on the basis of inadequate information. That same strategy would be wrong for a sustaining success or realignment situation, where the existing team has significant strengths that should be leveraged to meet new challenges.

Start-up

Start-ups pose several paired challenges and opportunities. While you will not be encumbered by old, broken structures, you will have to build structures and documentation from scratch. You can recruit your own team, but you will not have an experienced team to back you up. Your team will have to be mentored and fostered to develop the relationships, procedures, and lines of communication that will make it effective.

Turnaround

In a turnaround situation, it is likely that you are dealing with compressed time scales, limited resources, and a demoralized team. On the other hand, there will be a recognition that changes are necessary, and it is likely that you will be given the necessary support to implement those changes.

As your changes start to bear fruit, you will be able to build momentum and support quickly. People want to be part of successful teams. On the other hand, the pressure for early wins is higher in a turnaround situation than in

---

[3]Michael Watkins, *The First 90 Days* (Boston, MA: Harvard Business School Press, 2003).

the others. If you can't start making measurable progress right away, the organization will bring someone in to clean up the turnaround situation you will be leaving behind.

Realignment

In a realignment situation, you face a team that has been strong, but is no longer contributing to the organization's overall strategy. This type of situation can be tricky. On the one hand, there are strengths within the organization that can be used as a foundation for growth. But there are also engrained ways of thinking and acting that are no longer as productive as they once were. Your job will be to convince your team, your peers, your customers, and your boss that the team needs to move in a different direction.

Start-up and turnaround situations require immediate decisions and action, but realignments need some careful thought. You don't want to break what is working well. You also can't have your team wasting energy bucking against the organization's strategic direction.

Sustaining Success

This type of situation is both the easiest and the hardest type of environment to walk into. On the one hand, there is a strong culture in place that is accustomed to contributing to the health of the overall organization. On the other hand, it is very difficult to get the credibility to make the changes that will need to be made as the organization evolves. Complacency is a tough foe to vanquish.

Identifying Problems

As you build your team, keep an eye out for some common types of management failure. Be honest with yourself; if you have any of these problems, they will not go away on their own. It will require concentrated effort to overcome them. It will be easier to resolve these issues in your first 90 days than later. Spend the time and energy to resolve them now.

- **Unclear direction.** Your staff needs to understand what your priorities are, and how they fit into the overall organization's direction. When people don't understand the priorities, or why the priorities are what they are, they will waste a lot of time on unproductive work. When people understand why they are being asked to do something, they will be empowered to make the right decisions and to spend their energy in the right direction.

- **Living in the past.** It may be that your team is doing things that made sense some time ago, but don't match the way things are now. This is common in environments that have undergone significant growth, where people try to apply a small group mindset to a data center environment.

- **Complacency.** Things have been going okay, but people have stopped looking for ways to improve the environment. Your competition is not sleeping, and you should not be sleeping either.

- **Change fatigue.** Teams can only digest so much change at a time. If everything is changing at once, the team's members will lose focus. Mistakes and shoddy workmanship will result.

- **No consequences for poor performance.** A symptom of this is when there are a lot of oddball reporting relationships that are left in place to avoid hurting peoples' feelings. Sometimes demotions are necessary. They aren't easy, and should not be undertaken without trying to mentor the person to fix the problem. On the other hand, you cannot tolerate poor performance, or your good performers will not see the incentive to keep pushing.

- **Inadequate delegation.** When managing a turnaround situation, or when training inexperienced staff, the manager may need to be more involved in the beginning. But the expectation needs to be that the manager manages by delegating work to the team members, and the team members execute the work. The lines get muddied a bit if you are expected to be a "working manager" or "team lead" for a small group, but delegation is important. Assign responsibility along with the task, and try to foster a sense of ownership among your team members.

- **Unclear communication.** Set expectations, set them clearly, and set them in a standard way. Follow up and ask questions to ensure that the team member understood what you were asking for. Track assignments, and make sure that deliverables come back with what you expected.

Selecting Your Early Wins

When you are planning out your early wins, it is important to recognize that they are stepping stones into the future. You have to pick early wins that will be templates for what you want to accomplish and how you want to accomplish it in the future.

You can't improve everything at once. Focus is important, so you will need to pick wins that matter, either in isolation or as part of a larger win that is coming later. If you spread your attention across too many areas of focus, you are not focusing on anything.

Wins should be something that matters both to your plans and to the overall organization. Emphasize to your team that business alignment is a key part of measuring success.

If your boss or the organization culture does not recognize your wins as important, they will not garner you the credibility you need. That is why it is critical that you sell your proposed wins to your boss as part of your 90-day plan, and that you are selecting things that will be seen as legitimate wins within your team and throughout the organization.

The process is important too. If you accomplish the goal, but you don't use it to set up the processes you want, you have wasted an opportunity. Early wins are important for building momentum, team morale, and credibility, but they are most important for setting up future changes in processes, strategy, skills, and structure in future waves of change. Early wins have to be selected and executed with the bigger picture in mind. Early wins are most valuable as learning opportunities. The tasks leading up to the wins are your opportunity to get the team working together the way you need them to work together going forward.

As you are selecting items for early wins, look for structural, strategic items that can be put in place to make your team work more effectively. If you can implement something to replace or optimize manual processes that will pay off in spades later on.

Your Team's Transition

Your direct reports will need to work with you in your new role. Help them to make the same transition you are making with your own boss.

The steps are basically the same as what you need to carry out with your boss, but in reverse. Make things easier for them. Reach out, schedule time, and make yourself available. Structural items such as regular planning meetings in small groups can help create the team identity you are trying to create.

Get to know your team members, and let them know that they are valued. Identify their strongest characteristics, compliment them on those characteristics, and think of ways that you can assign work to take advantage of their strengths.

Everyone likes to be valued; value your employees. Make them look good, and they will make you look good.

Communicate your expectations clearly. Be fair. Be available. Be the kind of boss you would like to have.

The New Boss's To-Do List

Helping your people get used to you involves a lot of the same things that we listed earlier on how you should learn to work with your new boss:

- **Stay in touch.** Make yourself accessible to your team members, and schedule time with each of them. You will need to spend a lot of time with them early so they can learn how you like things done.

- **Teach them that they can trust you with problems.** Nobody likes to report a problem to the boss. Don't shoot the messenger. Teach your team that you want to have problems reported to you. But also teach them that you want them to report possible solutions at the same time they report the problem ("I see XYZ, and I think ABC would help").

- **Learn your people's working styles, and learn to fit them into your team's work.** Different personality types are needed for different types of tasks; assign work intelligently.

- **Take responsibility for the relationship.** Don't let resentments fester. Discuss them. You are the boss, and never forget it. That doesn't mean you are perfect, or that all the decisions you make are optimal. Learn to listen, and consider what is said. You may not agree with it, but most people appreciate being heard out, even if the decision goes against them.

- **Lay out expectations and priorities clearly.** This includes timelines, as well as concrete deliverables.

- **State your untouchables clearly.** You have some bottom lines about what you expect, things that you will not compromise on. Communicate those clearly and explicitly, and label them as nonnegotiable.

The 90-Day Plan

Your 90-day plan will be a living document. Include your early wins, as well as the steps you are taking toward the longer-term changes you will put into place. Include your learning plan, and report the results to your boss.

Throughout your first 90 days, update your plan and review it with your boss. Make sure your boss understands what wins you have logged, what challenges you have overcome, and what plans you have for facing other challenges within the organization.

The exact format for your 90-day plan depends on what you and your boss decide is a good way to capture your observations and goals. It could be a spreadsheet, or a project plan, or a text document. The key is that it captures and documents your priorities for your critical first 90 days.

You will probably want to have a few different versions of your 90-day plan. These can be maintained by using a filtering function on a spreadsheet or a project plan, or they can be separate documents. You may want to keep versions of your 90-day plan for different audiences.

- **Yourself.** This can be the most detailed version of your plan, and can include specific action items for developing your relationship with different team members.

- **Your boss.** This version should be geared toward the meetings you have with your boss to track your progress. Your boss does not want to know every detail, just your progress toward your goals, and the areas where you need air cover, a decision, or executive support.

- **Your team.** Your team should understand where you plan on taking them. State and restate your goals. Publish them. Make sure that your plan reflects your priorities, and then engage your team to work the plan.

- **The organization.** Your peers and other related groups need to understand what direction you are going. Sell them on the advantages of what you are doing, and publish your progress, so they can see what your team is working toward.

The 90-day plan can provide a focus and agenda for your regular discussions with your boss. It will help keep you aligned with what the boss wants, the organization needs, and what you want to accomplish as the leader of your team.

Summary

Here are a few ideas of questions you should think about when drawing up your 90-day plan:

- What are the gaps between what my team is doing now and what the company needs?

- Which of these gaps have a direct impact on client satisfaction?

- What skills or expertise does my team lack? What can we do about that?

- Where does my team lack depth? Who can be cross-trained to fill the gap?

- What structural changes do I need to make to my team?

Discussion Questions

1. What are the most important data to gather about your new position?

2. What questions will you ask of your new team members?

3. Where do you think your most significant challenges will arise?

4. Who have you seen make a smooth transition into a leadership position? What did that person do to ease the transition?

5. What is the most important thing you want to accomplish while leading your team?

6. What are the most important things you want your team members to accomplish?

Further Reading

Harvard Business Essentials. *Manager's Toolkit*. Boston, MA: Harvard Business School Press. 2004.

Watkins, Michael. *The First 90 Days*. Boston, MA: Harvard Business School Press. 2003.

Time Management

When you were a team member, you managed your own time. You probably did a pretty good job at it; you were effective enough to be seen as a leader. As a manager or team lead, you suddenly have a whole new set of challenges. Now you no longer manage just your own time; you have to make sure your direct reports' time is being used effectively as well.

The Multitasking Myth

Before you can help your employees conquer their time management demons, you have to vanquish your own.

The key to managing your time effectively is to develop good habits. You are a human being, and you have limitations.

As a techie, you are very familiar with what happens when a system context switches. When a computer switches contexts from one task to another, the CPU dumps its cache, loads the new context into cache, and starts scheduling tasks for execution. In a lot of ways, that is exactly what happens inside of your head when you are interrupted and are forced to context switch. You "lose track" of where you were in the original task, and you have to spend time syncing back up when you go back to what you were doing.

There is overhead associated with switching your mind-set to deal with the new task. You know that it is true, if you are honest with yourself. Study after study shows that context switching comes with a performance penalty, whether you are talking about a silicon or an organic computer.

Multitasking is a myth. At best, you are time slicing, where you move rapidly between tasks, pushing each of them just a little further along. Because of the context-switching overhead, it takes longer to get everything done with multitasking than if you handle tasks sequentially.

The exceptions to the "no multitasking" rule are tasks that have a long lead time. Examples would be starting purchasing paperwork that will take a long time to complete, downloading large files, and requesting information that won't come back for a while. In those cases, get the tasks kicked off, set reminder tasks for yourself to follow up, and move on to something else.

It would be a beautiful world if you could somehow schedule all your work to run sequentially. Good luck with that. I've never seen an environment where that was actually possible. But you can control how frequently you have to switch contexts. That is a huge win all by itself.

You are going to face interruptions. That is reality, so we have to develop habits and techniques to work around interruptions.

Scheduling, Calendars, and To-Do Lists

Before you can get your arms around how to schedule your day better, you have to be honest about what you actually do. One technique is to log your time every few minutes through a "typical" business day. The data you gather can help you identify where your time is actually going.

As human beings, we spend an astonishing amount of time trying to remember the next task we need to work on and prioritize our work. Two tools have been time tested and proven to help you organize your work: calendars and to-do lists.

Before you go too far, you need to designate a single repository for your scheduling information. Modern technology is wonderful. It is relatively easy to set up a computer-based calendar that will sync to your phone (or PDA), so the same calendar and to-do information is available to you on multiple platforms, wherever you are. If you work around this capability by setting up multiple calendars and to-do lists, you are just working against yourself.

The real key is to develop habits. You should have a routine every day that involves reviewing the work for today on the calendar and your to-do list. This routine needs to become a habit that you execute without even thinking about it.

Calendars

Your office probably has a calendaring standard. It makes the most sense to adopt this standard, because it will let you check other peoples' schedules when you are setting up meetings and appointments. Sync this calendar to your handheld device one way or another; you always need your calendar with you.

Make sure that your calendar reflects your priorities. Each day, look at what is on your calendar. If there are meetings or items that do not align with your priorities, arrange to move, cancel, or redefine them.

To-Do Lists and Ticketing Systems

To-do lists are different from calendars. You have a certain number of high-priority tasks that have close deadlines, but no specific time associated with them. Where possible, move these tasks onto either your calendar or one of your subordinates' calendars. (If you delegate a task, you need to add a task for yourself to follow up and check the status.)

To be effective, to-do lists need to be short. They also need to be reviewed every day. Block out time every day at the beginning of the day to structure your to-do list. Move tasks onto a calendar, and prioritize the tasks.

The key here is to develop a habit of setting up your to-do list every day, as your first task. This may mean that you process it before you travel into the office, or it may mean that you kick everyone out of your office or cube for the first 10 minutes you are at work. This has to be part of your daily schedule, and it has to be right at the beginning.

Priorities

The key to a successful to-do list of any sort is prioritization. There are a few different schemes for prioritizing things, but sometimes simplest is best.

The two most useful and flexible ways to prioritize are either to list items in strict priority order or to assign items to priority buckets (P1, P2, P3, etc.).

Priority lists are usually most useful when considering a relatively small number of items. For a handful of items, it is useful to decide in what order the items will be addressed. But when you get to more than ten items or so, comparing the relative merits of every two items on the list starts to take more time than it is worth.

For longer lists of items, it can help to sort them into buckets. This will only work if you take a very hard look at items that are categorized as P1 and P2. Most items need to be categorized P3 or below.

You can assign priority definitions as is useful in a particular case. Some common definitions would be as follows:

- **P1.** Needs to be addressed immediately. (For example, a customer-facing production system is down and needs to be recovered.)

- **P2.** Needs to be addressed as soon as possible. (For example, a system has a failing component, and maintenance needs to be scheduled in the next available maintenance window.)

- **P3.** Urgent, but can be scheduled in conjunction with other priorities.

- **P4.** Important, but can be scheduled when convenient.

- **P5.** Planning and analysis underway to determine an appropriate priority.

Ticketing Systems

The best to-do list is a ticketing system.

- It is easy to delegate tasks by assigning them to someone's queue.

- You can track completion and progress. (A key to that is to enforce discipline on people keeping their ticket queues in shape.)

- Customers can assign you tasks without walking over and interrupting you.

- Your boss can see what you are doing.

- It allows people to schedule tasks in an optimal way, rather than working on an interrupt basis.

If you can get the discipline of a ticketing system going, it will save tremendous amounts of time. If you do not have a ticketing system in place, this needs to become part of your 90-day plan.

There are many structural advantages to having a ticketing system. Customers know that they can make a request, and it won't be forgotten or buried. There is accountability because you know exactly how long it has been since the ticket was opened or actioned. And it becomes very easy to run reports to see what peoples' workload is, and what they are working on.

Every good boss I have worked for has needed a way to check on what my team is doing. A ticketing system allows us to set up a canned report that he can click on to see workload, outstanding tasks, and which team members have accomplished what tasks in the last week. This is a huge time saver for everyone, and totally removes the need for me to spend hours generating reports on peoples' activity.

And because we are disciplined about adding all our work into the ticketing system, it becomes much easier to write up annual reviews, because I can generate a summary of tickets completed to remind myself what each person worked on.

Here are the keys to making the ticketing system work for you rather than being just one more chore:

- Every person reviews his assigned tickets at least twice during the day, at the beginning and near the end of the day.

- Every task that takes more than a few minutes to execute gets a ticket. (If your ticketing system takes more than a few seconds to open a ticket, that is a serious problem that needs to be addressed.)

- The team's outstanding active tickets are reviewed once a week between the team manager and each team member. If there are obstacles, additional tasks are opened to clear them.

- Tickets are marked "resolved" when we believe the work is complete. This notifies the customer that the work is complete. The ticket is not "closed" (i.e., made so that it cannot be re-opened) until either the customer confirms that the work is good, or a defined time period has passed without a response from the customer.

- Work progress is tracked in the ticket.

- Emails about the task include the ticket number for reference. (Our ticketing system can be cc'd on the email, so that the email stream itself is logged into the ticket.)

Scheduling To-Do Items

When you review your to-do list (ticket queue), you should be able to estimate approximately how long each task will take, and what its priority is. Use that information to schedule work for the day, delegate as much as you can, and postpone some of it to tomorrow's list.

Priority is not just a matter of working the most important stuff first. Sometimes you will want to group items together into clusters with shared elements. If you can knock off two jobs with overlapping requirements, that is a good thing, as long as one of those jobs is high on your priority list.

Given a list of tasks, it takes the same amount of time to do them in any order. If you can do them in an order based on their priority, you will be perceived as working faster and better. This is an important life lesson. Work the tasks in priority order, and you will be more effective in the same amount of time.

Time Killers

Emergencies come up, and they will kill your schedule when they do. That is reality, but it is also an excuse. There are a few time killers that are common across a lot of managers:

- **Overreaching.** You have gotten as far as you have because you are able to get a lot done. But if you take on too many tasks, your effectiveness nosedives.

- **Reverse delegation.** It is very common for a manager to be overwhelmed while the subordinates have slack capacity. This is a symptom that tasks are not being delegated to the subordinates properly, or that the tasks are bouncing back onto the manager.

- **Time wasters.** There are a lot of little time wasting habits that add up to significant time over the course of the day. If you are honest when you create your time log, you will find out what your particular time wasting sins are.

Here's a quick look at how to deal with each of these.

Overreaching

There is always more work to be done than time to do it. That doesn't mean that you have to commit to doing all of it right now. You are a manager. Prioritize.

You may not have the information you need to prioritize effectively. Use your subordinates. Assign one of them the task of gathering the information you need so that you know what requirements surround a particular task. What is driving the urgency? What is involved in fulfilling the request?

Be specific about what you are asking the subordinate to gather, otherwise you will just waste time and energy repeating the exercise all over again.

Reverse Delegation and the Clinging Monkey Problem

A classic business analogy is of a problem being a monkey on someone's back. When you delegate a task, you put the monkey on the subordinate's back.

When an employee hits a snag, he or she may properly come back to the manager to discuss the problem and get advice. A common mistake managers make is to take the problem back away from the subordinate. That is a self-defeating strategy, because soon the manager is doing all the hard tasks assigned to the team, while the subordinates run out of important work to do. That is poor management of the team's bandwidth.

If you take back the monkeys, you do several things:

- You set up a dynamic where the manager is personally executing all the hard tasks.

- You create an environment of dependency, where your subordinates lose faith in their own abilities to resolve problems.

- You slow down the entire group's work because you are executing tasks rather than managing the team.

You have a full-time job already, running the team. You need to empower your subordinates to execute their jobs and to resolve the outstanding problems.

Why Do Managers Take Back the Monkeys?

- Technical managers may well be able to execute the task more quickly and better than less experienced team members.

- It may take less time on a particular task for the manager to just execute it than to enable the employee to execute it.

- Managers like the sense of power and control that comes from executing the tasks.

Maybe you can do the task faster and better than a more junior team member, but that isn't the end goal here. Most problems are not one-time problems; you will keep seeing the same type of problem coming back repeatedly. If you can train a subordinate to take care of that problem effectively, it will disappear from your plate.

Your more junior employee becomes more capable, an entire class of problems becomes easier to handle, and the bandwidth of your team expands when you teach your junior team members to handle a problem effectively.

It takes discipline to break the habits of a professional lifetime and leave the monkey on your employee's back.

Your team members need to understand what you are doing, because they are probably aware that you can execute the task faster and better than they can. You can even use the language of the monkey and explicitly tell them that when they come into your office with a monkey, they have to take the monkey back out the door with them.

It is appropriate for team members to upward delegate a task that requires you to use your authority as the team lead. This is different from them asking you to resolve the problem or take ownership of it.

An example would be when there is a political obstacle that is happening at a level above your team member, and you need to speak to a corresponding manager or even delegate upward to your own boss.

When you accept an upward delegation, make sure that your team member understands that he or she is still accountable for the overall task. Then take care of your part quickly so that your employee can get back to work.

That is different from throwing the team member into the deep end of the pool and hoping he or she can swim. Hear your employee out. Maybe there is a legitimate problem that is preventing progress on the problem. See if you can help identify a solution. If more research or information is needed, help your subordinate identify where the information lives, and how to get it. You may have to help the employee drill down a couple of levels to get to where there is a substantive task the employee can execute to push the problem forward.

If there is a query or request that needs to go out under your name for some reason, let the subordinate draft the request so that you can forward it, with the employee cc'd. In the request, specify that the subordinate is the owner of the problem, and explicitly state that responses need to go to him or her.

These techniques may seem like they take a lot of time, and they do. But you have to be disciplined enough to leave the monkeys on your team members' backs so that you don't end up with the entire zoo on yours.

Time Wasters

Your log should help reveal where your time is actually going. Here are a few common time wasters:

- Paperwork for the sake of paperwork.
- Meetings with no purpose or no direction.
- Visitors who are just hanging out.

- Phone calls that aren't about the task at hand.

- Procrastination.

- Lost efficiency during travel.

- Watching the email queue.

- IM/Twitter/RSS feeds/web surfing.

Together, these can eat up significant amounts of time. As each problem is recognized, it can be attacked. For a lot of these, you know what the answer is already; you don't need me to tell you.

Some tasks can be delegated. Some can be automated. For that matter, the task of automation can be delegated.

Paperwork

Paperwork is a good example. If you are filling out the same paperwork over and over, you should be able to find a way to use a template or a script to take care of it for you.

We already discussed the idea of using the ticketing system to help you produce activity and progress reports. Use that idea for other types of paperwork too.

A frequent type of paperwork involves inventory, whether it be for planning purposes, billing, or support renewals. Make sure your environment is inventoried on a database that is easily accessible. Enforce the discipline in your team of keeping it up to date. Inventory updates need to be part of the standard procedures for adds/moves/changes. Assign tasks for regular verifications of the inventory.

If you keep your central database up to date, it becomes much easier to pull reports on the types of information you need when that maintenance renewal comes up or you have to count how many systems need to be moved for that data center migration.

Meetings

If this is a meeting you are responsible for, either shape it up or cancel it.

Otherwise, check with the organizer to see what they expect from your team. Ask for the agenda. If the organizer has to assemble an agenda to respond to your question, so much the better. Your peers will also be grateful.

For a lot of meetings, there is no reason not to delegate them to one or more of your subordinates. Ask them to take notes and send you a summary. The only meetings you absolutely have to attend yourself are the ones discussing confidential information that your employees aren't authorized to have. Hopefully, there should not be too many of those.

Phone Calls

Nobody says that you have to take every phone call or chat with every visitor. Let some of the calls roll onto voicemail; you can add the important ones to your to-do list. Caller ID is a wonderful thing.

Procrastination

You know you shouldn't do that, right? Problems don't get smaller over time—at least they don't for me.

Develop a method and habits for dealing with incoming work. Put the work on a schedule and a to-do list, and execute it. You'll spend less time just doing the work than you would avoiding it.

Office Drop-Ins

Tell people in your office that you are working on something, and ask if you can get back to them later. If people have a legitimate question, you can assign a subordinate to gather the information and try to answer it.

Travel

Face-to-face meetings have a place, and are more time efficient than long distance meetings for some types of information transfer. But you have to take into account the amount of time and money spent during travel. Become effective at using conference and video calls, and recover all that time you used to spend hunting for an outlet in the airport.

Email

You should not be watching your email for incoming messages. I can guarantee that you have incoming messages all the time.

To manage your email (rather than having email manage you), you have to develop a strategy that works. Not all of these principles will work for you, but here are some ideas that have worked for others:

- Don't read your email before processing your to-do list (or ticket queue) in the morning. At most, scan the list for mails from your boss or with subject lines that indicate a real emergency, and then close the email client down until your to-do list is complete.

- When you process your mail in the morning, sort it by conversation, and process it by subject.

- Look for the most recent emails. If something is really hot, it is likely that there is current traffic on it.

- Look for mails from your boss. Your priorities are probably whatever your boss says they are.

- Don't leave the mail client running all day long. Schedule times during the day when you review your messages.

- Don't use email as a to-do list. If something needs action, open a ticket and paste the email into it. Then assign the ticket to the right person for follow up.

Don't be part of someone else's email problem. There are a few guidelines you should follow to be a good email netizen:

- Be concise. Be simple. Be direct. Take the time to write an easily understood email in as few words as possible.

- Use bullet points or numbered lists to separate key action items.

- Request an action and a timeline for that action.

- Don't assume your email was actually read. Everyone else's email queue is probably as busy as yours.

- Separate out reference information into attachments or (better yet) links to the documentation repository. Keep the email down to the key action items.

- Consider making a phone call. Sometimes a quick phone call can resolve something faster than an afternoon of back-and-forth emails.

Most important, don't send the email if it doesn't need to be sent.

Surfing and Goofing Off

There is nothing wrong with goofing off, from time to time. But it needs to be structured, and should be used as a reward for accomplishing work. When surfing comes before you have reviewed your ticket queue, you are going to run into trouble.

You also have to be careful about the message you are sending. If you are surfing during regular working hours, your subordinates will think that they are free to do likewise. Define separation and have the discipline to stick to it.

Delegating Effectively

We already discussed the "clinging monkey" problem earlier in this chapter. A key principle to remember is that once tasks are delegated, they need to stay delegated. If you allow your team members to delegate tasks back to you, your team will not function properly. You will be completely overwhelmed, and your team will not be working to its potential.

There are several keys to effective delegation:

- **Set clear expectations.** This includes what you want done and when it must be done. Include all requirements about how the task must be done.

- **Make sure your team feels a sense of shared responsibility for the team's work.** This can be built by discussing the relationship of the team's work to organizational goals in the weekly staff meeting.

- **Try to spread the interesting tasks around the staff.**

- **Delegate some tasks that increase team members' visibility within the organization.**

- **Understand your subordinates' capabilities and interests.** Delegate appropriate tasks that the team members are able to handle, but allow them to learn and grow.

- **Provide coaching as needed.**

- **Delegate responsibility at a project or function level to encourage a sense of ownership.**

- **Follow up frequently to monitor progress.** Provide feedback and coaching as needed. Make yourself available if advice or instructions are needed.

Delegation is one of the most important tools in your tool chest. Like any tool, it can be abused.

Do not use delegation to get out of unpleasant tasks that really belong to the manager. Politically charged meetings or difficult negotiations are legitimately the province of the manager, though you may want to bring one of your senior people along to answer technical questions.

Above all, you cannot be seen as using delegation as a way of getting out of your work so that you can leave early. That sort of impression is a cancer that can eat your team's soul.

You may not be able to delegate certain tasks, and you will only be able to delegate a portion of other tasks. Part of your job as a manager is to analyze the projects and functions facing your team, split them up as needed, and assign them to the right people.

Do not delegate tasks that expose your team members to consequences that are not appropriate to their positions. For example, the following types of tasks should not be delegated:

- Tasks involving your management responsibilities toward other team members. (This includes items such as performance reviews.)

- Solo negotiations with external customers or suppliers.

- Tasks that require technical expertise that the team member does not have.

- Communicating hiring, firing, or disciplinary information to other team members.

As team members complete tasks, use their progress to provide feedback on how they did. If you don't provide explicit requirements up front and detailed feedback afterward, your team members won't be able to meet your expectations.

Managing Meetings

In general, there are two types of meetings that need to be cared for. Some meetings allow people to report status on outstanding tasks. Other meetings are for working on a problem.

Status meetings typically have a large attendee list, because everyone on a project has tasks that depend on the status of what other people are doing. The person running the meeting should keep it moving along, and should make a summary available (maybe on a shared folder or web page, maybe in an email) after the meeting. It is a waste of time to try to solve problems in a status meeting. If there is a problem, the few people involved should convene a working meeting.

A working meeting should only include people who are directly contributing to resolving the problem. It should be focused, and attendees should receive a problem summary prior to the meeting so that they can prepare suggestions or relevant information prior to the meeting. The person running the meeting needs to keep it focused on the task at hand. This may mean scheduling other working meetings for other tasks.

Review meetings for requirements, design, and code are frequently seen as a waste of time, but they actually save much more time than they cost. Of course, these meetings need to be run well to be effective.

When you are in charge of a meeting, distribute an agenda beforehand, arrive on time, start on time, stick to the agenda as far as possible, and send a summary afterward. If something needs further discussion, schedule a breakout session to deal with it.

Is a meeting necessary? Sometimes it can take a long time to discover a convenient meeting time to work out a relatively simple problem.

If a phone call or email can resolve the issue, use that instead of a meeting. It will save everyone's time, and things will get done quicker.

Communicate the resolutions properly. This communication may be in a status meeting, an email notification, or a status update to a project plan.

Make sure that your meetings are well-organized and focused:

- Only call meetings that are necessary, with a clearly stated purpose and intended outcome.

- Only invite people who need to be there. (Other people may be advised that the meeting is taking place, as appropriate.)

- Provide an agenda before the meeting, with ample time for participants to request clarifications or changes to the agenda.

- Make logistical arrangements. Depending on the nature of the meeting, this may include a meeting room, a conference bridge, a WebEx session, a projector for an introductory presentation, handouts, or refreshments.

- Run the meeting professionally. This includes introducing participants (if needed), stating the purpose for the meeting, and laying down the ground rules before starting on the agenda. Participation should be encouraged, but the schedule should be kept. Breakout or follow-up meetings may be scheduled as needed. Minutes are distributed shortly after the meeting, including only critical issues and decisions addressed in the meeting.

Chapter 9 contains some tools that can help with troubleshooting and discussing problems. Not every one of those tools is useful for every situation. But sometimes something like an Ishikawa fishbone diagram can help organize the discussion in a productive way. Learn the tools and they can help you run a more effective discussion quicker.

The Art of Facilitation

Some meetings will involve hashing out a contentious issue. If you are hosting a meeting like this, don't let the meeting get away from you. Establish the agenda early on, and stick with it. Sit in a dominant position in the room (maybe near the white board, maybe at the most visible position on the table).

Listen to the ideas that are presented, but move the conversation along. Get to the kernel of what is being suggested, note it, and move along.

In some meetings, part of the agenda may be to establish which options are being considered. Rather than jumping right into the consideration phase, take the first part of the meeting to get a list of the options under consideration.

Structure the remainder of the meeting to discuss each of these options in turn. Make sure that the proponents of the different options know that their turn is coming, perhaps by posting a list of the options and the order in which they will be considered. Use a similar analysis framework for each option (pro/con lists work pretty well in most situations) so that everyone feels that each option has received due consideration.

Meetings of this sort usually break down when someone feels that their point of view is not being represented or considered respectfully. It may be helpful to meet with some of the proponents one-on-one beforehand so that they understand that they will be heard. (Their idea may not be adopted, but at least it will be considered respectfully.)

Keep the meeting on pace so that there is time to consider each option on the list. Stick to the schedule. If the schedule is not going to work, schedule breakout or follow-up meetings for options that need more work or more consideration.

End the meeting on a high note, even if the only thing agreed to is the type of analysis that needs to be done and the questions that need to be answered.

Traffic Cop

One key to productivity on a technology team is allowing team members to concentrate on a task for significant amounts of time. In a world of constant interruptions, that can be difficult.

The interruptions will never go away. The nature of IT is that there are a lot of small tasks that can be done quickly. But if the whole team is in constant interrupt mode working on these small tasks, the big ones never get done.

A way to deal with this is to schedule different people on the team into a traffic cop role at different times during the day. The traffic cop can look over incoming requests, ensure the requests are in a properly formatted ticket, take care of the quick hits, and possibly assign the longer tickets to the appropriate team member.

By spreading the traffic cop role around the team, most of the team should be able to work uninterrupted on the tasks that need concentration and attention.

You can look at which of your team members seem to work best at different times of day, and assign the traffic cop role to appropriate people during different shifts.

On-Call Scheduling

On-call scheduling is something that nobody likes, but that is necessary for a well-functioning environment. There are a few principles to keep in mind when drawing up an on-call schedule.

- **Be fair.** Everyone can count, so it becomes very obvious if someone is stuck on-call for an unusually large number of holidays or 3-day weekends.

- **Schedule in advance.** Give everyone lots of notice of the on-call schedule, so that they can make plans or arrange to swap on-call shifts if needed.

- **Allow flexibility.** Let team members arrange with each other to swap on-call schedules if necessary. Encourage team members to be generous, but ask them to handle exchanges among themselves. If someone starts to take advantage of teammates, call the person aside and discuss it.

- **Be humane.** When someone has late night or weekend on-call, allow them some flexibility to work reduced hours during the work week if they spend a lot of time working issues after hours.

Whether you should schedule yourself on-call depends on the size of your group and the scope of your responsibilities. If you are the technical lead for a team of equals, you should probably assign yourself an equal share of on-call duty. If you are expected to be the point of escalation for your team, it makes sense for you to have less onerous on-call duties, or even no regular on-call (as you are effectively on-call most of the time anyway).

If you are a team manager with full-time duties that are very distinct from the rest of the team, on-call may not make sense for you. If you are not hands-on as much as you used to be, you are more likely to make mistakes when responding to an incident.

The key is to be fair and to be ethical. Some team leads see their position as a way to get out of extra work or unwanted work. That is not the way to look at things. Your team members are not stupid. They will see such leaders as being lazy, and will lose respect for them.

When your team needs to report an incident after hours, you will probably be involved in any case. You may need to report it upwards in the hierarchy, or you may need to approve an emergency change. Make yourself available to the on-call person, and respect their time as far as possible.

The on-call schedule needs to be published in a well-known location for other teams to be able to use it. A wiki or something similar is a reasonable place to put it, or possibly a spreadsheet on a shared drive.

Ideally, there should be a common place where all the teams store their contact information, because you will need theirs as much as they need yours.

Summary

Time management is a critical skill for a new leader. Your team will take their cues from you. If they see someone who makes effective use of time, they will follow your example. If they see a hypocrite or an ineffectual boob, they will either lose respect or lose the sense of urgency that makes a successful team go.

Discussion Questions

1. What are your particular time management sins? What can you do to correct them?

2. Who is someone whose effectiveness you admire? How does that person organize his or her time?

3. Which is the most effective meeting you attend? What elements make it effective?

4. How much time do you spend doing similar tasks over and over? How could you make that process more efficient?

Further Reading

Berkun, Scott. *Making Things Happen*. Sebastopol, CA: O'Reilly, 2008.

Blanchard, Ken, and Spencer Johnson. *The One Minute Manager*. New York, NY: William Morrow, 2003.

Harvard Business Essentials. *Manager's Toolkit*. Boston, MA: Harvard Business School Press, 2004.

Limoncelli, Thomas A. *Time Management for System Administrators*. Sebastopol, CA: O'Reilly, 2005.

Oncken, Jr., William, and Donald L. Wass. *Management Time: Who's Got the Monkey?* (Harvard Business Review, OnPoint Enhanced Edition). Boston, MA: Harvard Business School Press, 2000.

Schwalbe, Kathy. *Information Technology Project Management*. Boston, MA: Thompson, 2006.

Project Management

As your team's leader, you will be responsible for projects and for tasks within projects. You may also assign projects for your subordinates to manage.

Project management is a discipline all to itself. It increases the number of successful projects (i.e., projects that are on time and within budget) by using a disciplined, industry-standard framework for running projects.

A project has several characteristics that make it different from day-to-day operations. Operational tasks are recurring tasks that are required to keep the environment in good working order. A project, on the other hand, is a temporary undertaking with a specific defined goal.

The key word in that definition is *goal*. If the goal is not defined, approved, and published, the project is guaranteed never to succeed. Without a defined goal, a project will become a Christmas tree, where everyone who wants anything will hang their particular ornament. In the world of project management, this is known as *scope creep*.

The other key in the definition of a project is that it is temporary, with a well-defined beginning and end. Because we are working toward a concrete goal that goal will be accomplished, and the project will end.

When running a project, the overall goal has to be divided up into bite-sized tasks. These tasks are assigned to a team or an individual for completion. We also map out the *dependency relationships* between the tasks (i.e., which tasks are dependent on the outcome of a previous task). Understanding the dependency relationships between the tasks and the resources needed for each task is the key to drawing up budgets for the money and time needed for the project.

What makes a project different from a task is that a project requires resources from several different people or groups. Coordinating these requirements is what a project manager does.

This chapter discusses many tools that are at the disposal of a project manager. Keep in mind that these tools are only useful as far as they help to achieve project goals. You can spend all your time fiddling spreadsheets without having a positive impact on the project. Everything you do needs to move the project closer to completion.

Note Project management is a much bigger topic than we can cover in one chapter. Please check into some of the references at the end of the chapter for a more complete view.

Setting Expectations

A project's size, usually known as its *scope*, has to be set as a defined, reasonable objective. A published scope, with measurable objectives, is the key to managing expectations from the people who depend on the project.

Project expectations are governed by the constraints of project management:

- **Capability.** The number and size of the deliverables in the project objective.

- **Time.** How long (in calendar time) it will take to complete the project scope.

- **Cost.** This includes both monetary costs as well as indirect costs (such as staff time or other resources).

- **Quality.** How reliable and robust the system is.

Part of defining a project's scope is identifying which of the constraints is the highest priority for the project's sponsor. You can't have a project be cheap and fast and still have it be feature rich. There is a balancing point in there somewhere that meets the needs of the organization.

Project management is not quite that simple. Drawing up and agreeing to the project objectives is a process all by itself. We try to maximize the project's usefulness by negotiating with the different stakeholders in the project.

PROJECT ROLES

Here are several roles that are important when setting up a project:

Project Champion. This person is someone high in the organization who is a key proponent of the project. Strong commitment to a project by a champion is a good predictor of project success. A champion can help corral needed approvals, resources, and attention to move a project along.

Project Sponsor. This person provides the leadership and political juice to move the project forward. The project sponsor will provide the funding and have the ultimate say on the direction of the project.

Project Manager. This person coordinates the work involved in the project, and makes sure that the project milestones are being achieved within time and budget constraints.

Project Team. Project tasks are assigned to different members of the project team.

Stakeholders. Stakeholders are the people who have an interest in the project. This includes customers and implementers of the project, as well as those funding it. The stakeholder community will have different interests. One of the challenges a project manager faces is balancing the different demands from the stakeholder community.

Project Phases

Part of the nature of projects is that they have distinct phases. One common way of designating these phases is represented by Figure 4-1:

| Concept | Design | Implementation | Closeout |

Figure 4-1. Project phases

- **Concept.** This is the phase where an idea is crystallized with preliminary estimates and feasibility studies. This phase should include preliminary timelines and cost estimates based on an agreed project scope.

- **Development.** In this phase, the project plan is developed and improved. The task list should be detailed thoroughly, and a budgetary cost estimate should be approved.

- **Implementation.** In this phase, the project is executed according to the plan. Progress is measured and tracked, and stakeholders are kept in the loop.

- **Closeout.** Once the implementation work is completed, the customer needs to accept the work. Postmortem sessions and reports should also be completed in this phase.

Figure 4-1 is appropriate for many projects, but some projects are better suited to an *iterative model.* In an iterative model, the emphasis is on delivering chunks of functionality or prototypes on an accelerated schedule, then repeating the process until the business unit is satisfied with the results. Figure 4-2 diagrams an iterative model.

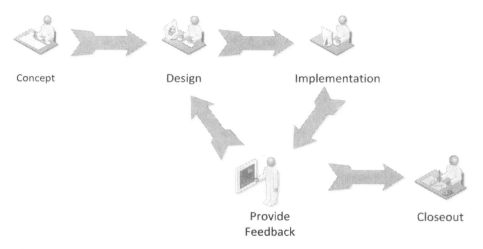

Concept   Design   Implementation

Provide   Closeout
Feedback

Figure 4-2. Iterative model

Iterative models are often *timeboxed*, meaning that the cycles have a defined length, usually only a few weeks.

There are several advantages to an iterative model:

- Progress is tangible and visible to the business unit.

- It provides a natural way to deal with evolving requirements as business needs change.

- Timeboxing provides a constant incentive to the development teams to produce.

- The most important functionality is usually delivered first. If the project runs out of time or resources, some business value will still have been provided before the project's end.

There also are some disadvantages:

- The structure of an iterative cycle can be used to excuse a failure to plan or architect properly.

- Discipline is needed to close out a project rather than allowing it to cycle endlessly.

Regardless of the approach, one of the best predictors of project success is if an organization follows a consistent process for initiating, reviewing, and executing projects. Failed projects can be hugely expensive for the organization. Having concrete phases and gate procedures is part of having a robust project management process to focus resources on business priorities.

Scope Definition

The project has to be defined. This includes defining the size of the project, as well as what the success criteria will be. Usually, a business case is drafted to justify the project's costs.

Part of defining the scope is identifying all the key stakeholders. The stakeholders must agree to the scope prior to beginning, and changes to the scope have to be accompanied with the resources to make those changes.

The initial scope of the project is defined and published in a document known as a *project charter*. The charter must be accepted by the key stakeholders; if a stakeholder is not on board that person or group may actively or inadvertently sabotage the project.

In many cases, it is best to finish the project with a limited scope, and then add features or functionality as part of a follow-up project. If a project manager does not control scope creep, the project is doomed to meander about and eventually fail when patience and resources are exhausted.

Business Case

A *business case* is exactly what it sounds like. It is a case made to management to secure the resources needed to pursue the project. A typical business case includes several elements:

- **Business objective.** What problem is being resolved by this project?

- **Current situation.** This may be presented in a SWOT format (Strengths, Weaknesses, Opportunities, and Threats).

- **Options.** Alternative ways of attacking the problem.

- **Recommendation.** Which one is preferred by the technical community? Why?

- **Project requirements.** What resources will be needed to accomplish the project?

- **Financials.** What is the preliminary budget? What is the estimated total impact of the project (costs and benefits)? The project manager should provide cost estimates for the expected lifetime of the project, not just the time to delivery. Budgeting is discussed further in Chapter 8.

- **Estimated schedule.** The schedule will be rough at this stage. Try to make it realistic. Base it on previous project experiences, if possible.

- **Known risks.** Include some proposed ways of dealing with these risks.

Organizations may have standard formats in which this information is expected to be presented, or methods that are used to estimate the financial impact. If you can look at a previous successful business case that may help format your business case the way that management likes to see it.

Project Charter

As its name suggests, the project charter is the document that kicks off a project. This document is a formal recognition of the project and its authority to call on the organization's resources to execute the project. The charter provides managerial direction for the objectives and management of the project.

Project charters should include the following:

- Project name and authorization date.

- Project manager's name and contact information.

- Schedule overview, based on the initial draft schedule.

- Budgetary guidance.

- High-level description of the project objectives.

- Summary of the approach planned for managing the project.

- List of roles and responsibilities.

Project charters may also contain additional comments or clarifications by stakeholders.

The charter is the founding document for the project. It is likely to be referenced repeatedly by those trying to affect the course of the project.

The level of detail in the charter is important. You don't want it to have too little detail, or different stakeholders will read their own preferences into the charter and insist on their own interpretation. Too much detail ties your hands and prevents you from doing what you need to do to bring the project in. The appropriate level of detail is going to depend on the project and the nature of the relationships between the different stakeholder groups.

Scope Statement

It is common for two *scope statements* to be produced during the early part of a project. Frequently, a preliminary scope statement (a "vision statement" or "scope charter") will be created from the project charter and circulated for discussion. A more detailed scope statement would be generated later to direct the project and to act as a control on scope creep.

The initial project charter is a very good place to start when developing the initial scope statement. The scope charter is likely to be high level, and is likely not to specify technical means required to achieve results.

There will be several scope statements circulated during the initial stages of the project. Each will become more detailed and will reflect the emerging consensus about what this project consists of.

There will always be pressure to expand the scope of a project. If the scope is allowed to grow too large, the project will lose focus and may never reach completion. There is a lot to be said for creating one project to create the base functionality and foundation for further growth. Additional features can be added as additional projects. Reducing the scope in this way increases the likelihood of success, and also cuts the time required to delivery meaningful functionality to the business.

When trying to decide what should be defined as base functionality, a good test is to look at the business impact of the different proposals. The key is to get significant business impact delivered quickly, in a way that will enable further enhancements to also be delivered efficiently.

STRUCTURING A SCOPE STATEMENT

Here is a common way to structure a scope statement. Depending on the complexity of the project, the "Requirements," "Product Deliverables," and "Success Criteria" sections may be split out into separate detailed documents. In that case, include a summary in the scope statement and a pointer to each detailed document.

Project Title: This is a unique name for the project. It is used to track project progress and costs in reports to management.

Document Version Number: This document will evolve over time. To see which version is current, a version number should be assigned to each version and incremented as the document is updated.

Date: The date the document was prepared by the project management team.

Prepared By: The name and contact information (including phone number and email address) for the project managers who prepared the document.

Project Justification: A brief one-paragraph description of why the project is necessary, including:

- *Who requested the project.*

- *A very brief description of what the project will accomplish.*

- *The rough estimated budget.*

Requirements: A numbered list of the requirements for the project. The initial list of requirements will probably be very general. The requirement specifications will become more detailed over the course of the project. Requirement numbers should not be re-assigned if requirements are retired; a requirement should keep the same reference number throughout the course of the project. If a requirement is removed, line it out rather than re-assigning its reference number.

Deliverables: This will be a list of what the project manager is committing to deliver as part of the project.

- *Project Management Deliverables*: The list of the project-management related material that the project manager will deliver throughout the project. Some common project management deliverables include: business case, charter, team contract (an agreement by each team to deliver required resources), scope statement, WBS (work breakdown structure, a structured task list), schedule, cost baseline, status reports, project presentation, project report, lessons-learned reports, and project budget.

- *Product Deliverables:* These are the deliverables that will specifically address the requirements. Deliverables should directly reference (by requirement number) which particular requirement they are fulfilling. As the scope document becomes more detailed, these deliverables will include specifications on what constitutes a successful delivery.

Success Criteria: Project completion within budget and on schedule are typical examples of success criteria. Special points of emphasis should be included here, such as specific milestones or deadlines that have a significant business impact.

Deliverables Postponed: When stakeholders agree to postpone a feature for a later version, keep track of the agreement. Otherwise, you will find yourself having the same discussion over and over, reminding people that the feature was postponed.

Scope Management

If you don't manage the scope, it will manage you. Every stakeholder has a distinct view of what the scope of the project should be. Once you have a preliminary scope statement in place, changes can only be permitted within the context of project change control.

The tools you have at your disposal to manage the scope are

- **Planning process.** This starts with deciding how the preliminary scope statement will be developed and evolve. Throughout the lifetime of the project, this planning process will have to be robust to define an achievable scope and filter proposed changes.

- **Task management.** As the scope develops, the *task list* or *work breakdown structure* (WBS) has to develop at the same time. If scope changes are not reflected and tracked in the WBS, project management will not focus on the correct issues.

- **Verification and control.** The scope change management process has to be robust, and project management has to be disciplined about enforcing its use. Stakeholders must agree to the downstream effects of project plan changes, including resource and schedule impacts of changes.

Each of these tools must be in place to manage a project's scope properly. An accurate WBS is impossible without a solid scope statement, and a stable scope statement only exists if the planning and control processes are also solid.

▓ **Note**   As part of the scope verification process, the completed project scope statement must be accepted by the stakeholders. Stakeholders need to agree to a clear change control process, including a strong *change control board* (CCB).

If you don't instill this discipline up front, you will spend a lot of time regretting it once you get into the meat of the project.

You have a few tools at your disposal to manage the scope, but political pressure will always be brought to bear to implement changes to the scope. There are a few different techniques you can use to combat scope creep. These would be used in conjunction with your change control process:

- **Cost.** Put a dollar amount on the resources required to implement a change, and ask the requestor and CCB to identify the budget the costs should be charged to. Once it comes down to budgetary dollars, people start getting serious about which scope changes are actually necessary.

- **Time.** Put a time on the delay that the request will cause to the project timeline. When people have to take responsibility for delaying the overall project deliverables, people become more flexible about the changes they are demanding.

- **Trade-offs.** Ask which existing requirement should be dropped to free up the resources needed to execute the change. There are always limited resources, and the most important items should be done first. By pitting requirements against each other, you force a decision about which priorities should be addressed first.

Stakeholders

Early in the project, a project manager needs to identify the stakeholders and decision makers. For each of the stakeholder groups, escalation procedures must be identified to deal with the unexpected.

Stakeholder management can be like herding cats. Different teams have different priorities. One of the more difficult tasks a project manager has is to identify a reasonable path forward that addresses all the most important stakeholder concerns without blowing either the budget or the timeline.

For anything beyond a simple project, project managers should produce a separate analysis of the stakeholders in the project. This should include information about organization and contact information for different stakeholder communities. It also may contain information about concerns about different stakeholder communities. This analysis probably should not be part of the public project management plan because some of the information may be confidential. The stakeholder analysis may only be shared among people directly responsible for managing the project, so that the project managers can feel comfortable communicating personal information about the stakeholders, and how to adjust the project management methods to fit their needs.

Team Contracts

Stakeholders will need to agree to team contracts. Depending on what is required from the stakeholder, the contract may include the following items:

- Agreement with the initial scope statement.

- A procedure by which changes are made to the project scope, requirements, or deliverables.

- Commitment to provide the resources specified in the project plan.

Work Breakdown Structure

One of the key coordination tasks for a project manager is the definition of a task list (sometimes called a work breakdown structure or *WBS*). The task list needs to identify a brief description of the task, the person (or group) responsible for the task, the approximate amount of time required to execute it, and the dependency relationships between tasks.

Specifications and requirements are not included in a WBS. A WBS only includes tasks; specifications and requirements are tracked separately. Because the requirements may affect the time estimates for a task, it is important to have the implementers review both the requirements and the time estimates.

The WBS is created by breaking down the project deliverables into smaller and smaller chunks. Each of these should continue to be decomposed until they arrive at the level of a task that is assignable and schedulable. These tasks at the lowest level of a WBS are sometimes called *work packages*. The amount of effort represented by a work package will depend on the length of the project and how frequently updates are required.

Resource and dependency scheduling will usually be handled at the work package level, so that is the level where the project manager needs to provide tracking and accountability. If weekly updates are needed to keep a multi-month project on track, for example, a work package should include no more than 40 hours of effort.

There are a number of tools that can be used to track task lists and dependency relationships. Microsoft Project is the best known of the commercial tools. There are also free tools such as GanttProject (http://www.ganttproject. biz/download) that have similar functionality, and can even save files in MS Project format. Some project managers prefer old-fashioned spreadsheets, but those can become unwieldy once the project grows past a certain size.

Whichever tool is used, the most important basic analysis is done at the task level. If you don't know what you want people to do, there is no way you are going to be able to estimate the resources you need to do it.

As you define the list of tasks, you will need to speak to the teams who will execute those tasks for estimates of the time they will need, the number of people they will need to commit, and the dependency relationships they have with other tasks. It is very common for one task to need to be split up into smaller tasks assigned to different groups.

Developing a WBS

A rule of thumb is that any project can be decomposed into 10–20 items. Each of these can be decomposed further until we get to a level where each item is a work package. This is an example of a "top-down" method for producing a work breakdown structure.

There are a few different approaches that project managers use to develop a WBS. Some of these include:

- **Analogy.** If you have a WBS for a similar project, that is a good starting place. The estimated and reported task durations also may be useful in coming up with schedules for the current project.

- **Top-down.** Starting with the high-level tasks, break these down into component pieces. This approach is best used by someone with a deep understanding of what needs to happen in the project, perhaps someone with a good implementation background.

- **Bottom-up.** Identify as many detailed pieces as possible, and collect these into groupings of high-level tasks. This approach can help develop buy-in from the implementation teams, and it is effective for some projects that represent a new way of doing things.

- **Mind mapping.** This is a technique that starts with an objective drawn in the center of a diagram, perhaps on a white board. Tasks needed to accomplish that objective are drawn as branches from the center, and subtasks are branches from those tasks. This is a good technique for brainstorming during early project meetings to try to capture the different requirements. See Figure 4-3 for an example of a mind map of a simple project.

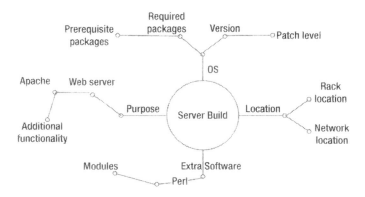

Figure 4-3. Mind map example of a simple project

Of necessity, several of the tasks will have descriptions that are telegraphic, if not vague. A WBS dictionary should be included to define what each task means. This is usually a document that is distributed with or linked from the WBS. The WBS dictionary may include links to the requirements.

WBS CONSTRUCTION

Here are a few principles to follow when constructing a WBS:

Uniqueness. Each work package appears only one place in a WBS.

Dependencies can be defined in the tool used to create the WBS. (This is much easier in a specialized tool such as Microsoft Project or GanttProject, as opposed to a spreadsheet.)

Nesting. Each WBS item consists exactly of the work packages below it in the WBS hierarchy. Dependencies should be tracked as dependencies, not by considering a work package to belong to two different hierarchies.

Accountability. Each WBS item belongs to a named person, even if some of the work packages are done by other people.

Consistency. The WBS needs to be consistent with how the work will actually be performed. The structure must be defined by reality, not aesthetics.

Buy-in. The project team has to be involved in constructing the WBS, to develop buy-in and ensure consistency.

Clarity. WBS items must be understandable. which probably means a definition in the WBS dictionary.

Flexibility. The WBS must be constructed in such a way that updates are doable. No matter how much planning and discussion is done up front, there will be changes. It is easier to implement these changes in a project management tool as opposed to a spreadsheet.

Resource Estimates

Throughout the project, the project manager is responsible for tracking the resources needed to bring the project to completion. This includes the people needed as well as the cost in dollars, facilities, and material. A preliminary estimate is drawn up before the project is approved, but the project manager has to keep a handle on the resource estimates as they change over the course of the project.

The basic tool for making the resource estimates will be the task list. Most projects have a large number of similar tasks; as each task is completed, you need to see if timelines for other tasks will need to be adjusted.

The advantage of a project management tool (rather than a simple spreadsheet or document), is that it will automatically adjust timelines and estimates based on changes to tasks in the plan. It will also help us view **critical path** changes.

The *critical path* is the name given to the path of tasks that is keeping the overall project from being any shorter.

Each task can be viewed as being part of a tree of dependency relationships, both of tasks that must be completed before this one, and also the tasks that are waiting for this one.

The critical path is calculated by looking at the durations of tasks in a dependency tree, and selecting dependency tree with the longest time duration.

This particular path is the "critical" path because if some of its elements can be shortened, the overall project time line can be shortened. Or, if one of its tasks is delayed, that will cause a delay in the overall project.

One of the earliest indicators of a project in trouble is when the resource requirements start to spiral up. It is the project manager's responsibility to track these requirements against what was approved for the project, and to alert project stakeholders if they start increasing in a way that puts the project in jeopardy.

As the WBS is completed, there will almost certainly be people who are assigned more tasks than they can possibly complete in the times assigned. When this happens, the project manager has a few tools that can be used:

- Identify tasks or parts of tasks that can be done ahead of time.

- Reschedule some tasks to different parts of the project plan, so that the person can focus on the more critical tasks first.

- Find ways to re-assign some of the work to other people, perhaps by bringing in temporary help.

It is a myth that more people means a faster project completion. There is overhead associated with managing new people and bringing them up to speed. Even when they are up to speed, there is additional communications overhead for each additional person.

Brooks' Law   Adding more people to a late project makes it later.

Brooks' Corollary   There is an incremental person who, when added to a project, slows down the project delivery.

Inaccurate Estimates

Estimation is not an easy skill to learn. When you find that your estimates are significantly off, you will need to find out what you are missing.

Many technical people dramatically underestimate the amount of time required for planning tasks such as sketching designs or attending planning meetings. Try to identify the types of things that are being missed in the estimates by asking clarifying questions. Once you identify someone's blind spots, help them to account for them in their estimates. It may be as mechanical as giving them a template including lines for the frequently overlooked items.

Schedule Estimates

For each task in the WBS, you need three numbers. You will need a best case, worst case, and most likely you will need to estimate for the amount of time needed for the task. These numbers will be used to perform scheduling estimates.

PERT analyses are a common way to provide schedule estimates. Appendix B provides some information on how to execute a PERT analysis.

Allow time for things to go wrong in the overall project schedule. Projects of any complexity will have something go wrong that will take more time. Programming in enough slack time without allowing the team to procrastinate and lose focus is an art, not a science. One way to do this is to add explicit WBS tasks under project management control for resolving variances.

THE OPTIMISM OF PROJECT TEAMS

Project teams tend to underestimate how long it will take to do something. This isn't because we are lazy or dishonest.

People who gravitate toward project work have a certain mindset. We like to accomplish something new. (Even better to accomplish something that everyone else thinks is impossible!) If we spent all our time thinking about what could go wrong, we would never finish the project, and we would probably never be invited to be a member of another project team.

When you are working on a schedule, question your assumptions. Are you assuming a best-case scenario? What unknowns could come back to clobber us? Make sure your schedule takes realistic estimates and risk assessments into account.

An overly precise schedule is an early indicator of problems in the project planning process.

Precision is very easy to achieve. Accuracy is much harder. You can spend a lot of time tweaking a schedule beforehand, but any nontrivial project schedule will need to be adjusted anyway as difficulties come to light.

Here are a few suggestions for improving the quality of your schedule estimates: How accurate should the task estimates be? Are you looking for a guess? A good estimate? A thorough analysis? You will want to focus more attention on tasks that are on the critical path or that are part of a lot of dependency chains. When you request an estimate from an implementation team member, you can ask for accuracy in terms of a confidence level. (Are you 50% sure? 80%? 90%?) Treat these numbers as a way to communicate expectations to team members, but take those numbers with a grain of salt. (Don't just use them for scheduling estimates because research shows that people routinely overestimate confidence levels.)

- **Don't ask for precise estimates of less important tasks.** If you chew up all your team's time making really good estimates, you will have less time to actually execute the project.

- **Trust the experts.** You can probably pressure the programmer to give you a smaller time estimate, but that doesn't mean that the work will actually take less time.

- **Provide accurate requirements.** You can analyze garbage to within an inch of its life, but you will still get garbage output.

- **Use previous project work as a baseline wherever possible.** Just understand where the information is comparable, and where it is not.

Project Requirements

The project scope is a general statement about the size of the project. Beyond that, stakeholders must agree to specific requirements and success criteria.

A *requirement* is a problem statement. It does not attempt to specify how the problem will be solved; it states the problem in a clear enough way that a knowledgeable person will be able to work toward a problem resolution. A good requirement statement is easy to understand, but hard to misinterpret.

Note *Requirement statements* are a form of communication. If they are not understood by both the requestor and the implementer, they need to be revisited.

Frequently, stakeholders will try to use these requirements to expand the scope of the project. The project manager must keep a handle on scope creep. If the scope needs to be expanded, stakeholders and decision makers have to allocate the resources to do so or reduce requirements elsewhere to free up the necessary resources.

Note Part of tracking requirements will be tracking the differences between the requirement statements and what actually comes out of the project. These differences are known as *variances*.

Variances need to pass through change control approval to be acceptable. Regardless, variances must be tracked and resolved as part of a successful project completion.

Software engineering makes a distinction between *C-requirements* (customer requirements) and *D-requirements* (developer requirements). C-requirements are usually high-level descriptions of behaviors that are wanted or needed; D-requirements are the specific, detailed requirements that developers use to implement the C-requirements.

There needs to be clear mapping between C-requirements and D-requirements. Standards that are based on the IEEE 930-1993 and 830-99 standards for expressing requirements use a unique identifying number for each requirement. For projects that have more than a trivial number of requirements, I recommend that you assign each requirement a number, that each D-requirement specifies a corresponding C-requirement, and implementation work packages reference a D-requirement. Otherwise, you will spend way too much time answering questions about why things are being done this way.

Note   In IEEE 930-1993 and 830-99, C-requirements are assigned 2.x numbers, while D-requirements are assigned 3.x numbers in a standard way. For example, subdivisions of "2.1.4" are used to express C-level software interface requirements; subdivisions of "2.1.5" describe C-level communications interfaces, etc.

If your organization has a standard way of expressing requirements, use it. If not, you can do a lot worse than downloading the 930-1993 and 830-99 standards from IEEE and using them as a template for assigning requirement numbers.

Requirements should be expressed in a standard way:

- Assign a unique identifying number to each requirement, preferably as part of a numbering structure that makes sense.

- Each requirement needs a brief descriptive name.

- The requirements should be published and easily findable. This means that the specifications document should be in a well-known location, and it should be structured so that specific types of requirements are easy to find.

- Requirements should be accompanied by tests to verify them. (Some methodologies define the requirements based on the tests required to verify them.)

- Requirements should point at the code sections or work packages that implement them, and vice versa.

Testing results should be indexed by the requirement number. That way, we can identify tests to validate each requirement, including unit, integration, and system-level tests.

LIST ASSUMPTIONS EXPLICITLY

Which project goals have not been made explicit in the documentation?

Which disagreements between team members may delay the project?

What are the underlying architecture and technology infrastructure?

Which standards or other organization requirements must be met?

Are there regulatory requirements that must be fulfilled?

Which expected organizational changes might impact the project estimates or team structure?

Are the definitions clear?

Have all the different teams been represented in the planning discussions?

Obtaining Requirements

Requirements can come out of interviews or workshop sessions. Sometimes requirements can be gathered by directly observing business processes. Gathering requirements is a skill that is developed over time. Professionals who gather business requirements for implementation are frequently known as *business systems analysts*.

There are several techniques that can be used to identify and nail down requirements:

- **Mock-up.** A *mock-up* is a nonworking model of a project component, usually used to demonstrate user interface functionality.

- **Prototyping.** A *prototype* is a working model of a component of the overall system. This method is especially useful for getting buy-in to interface requirements, because the input can be restricted or output canned to reflect look-and-feel types of operation. As components become more developed, they can be placed in a test harness to see how they would integrate into the whole.

- **Use cases.** *Use-case modeling* is a technique for identifying the steps that would happen as a system handles a typical operational case. This is less mechanistic than the way that a lot of techies look at how the system should operate, but use cases are accessible to most stakeholders, and they still provide a useful level of detail to the technical staff.

- **Joint application design (JAD).** This is a method that involves intense, structured workshops including all the stakeholders to try to bring out all the requirements. JAD brings the user community representatives into the requirements process in a focused way, which helps to increase their involvement and buy-in.

Beyond gathering requirements, you also need to get a feeling for how important each requirement is. Are they based on wants or needs? As the project progresses, there will be times you need to adjust the scope of the project, and it is best to know which parts of the scope have some flexibility in them.

Use cases, in particular, are a really useful way to gather C-level requirements at a useful level of detail. The information in a use case should include:

- **Use case ID:** Unique identifying number, preferably mapping to a C-level requirement.

- **Summary:** Verbal description of the use case.

- **Rationale:** Why the use case is needed.

- **Actors:** Groups of people or external systems that interact with this use case.

- **Initial state:** What needs to be in place at the beginning of the use case.

- **Actions:** The course of events in the use case.

- **Alternate paths:** Conditions where a similar, but not identical, course of actions would take place. (This allows us to collapse several similar, related use cases into one.)

- **Final state:** The status at the end of the use case.

These can be diagrammed in UML format (see Chapter 13), or they can be written out verbally, as in Example 4-1.

EXAMPLE 4-1: USE CASE EXAMPLE

ID: 2.2.2.1

Summary: Submit personal information in web form

Rationale: Web interface selected as most appropriate way to accept personal information

Actors:

1. End user with web browser

2. System: Web/application server

3. System: Database server

Initial state: End user has main web page displayed on web browser

Actions:

1. User selects "enter personal information" button from main web page

2. System displays personal information dialog box

3. User enters information

4. User pushes "submit" button

5. System writes data to user's database record

6. System displays "success" dialog box

7. User pushes "OK" button

8. System displays main web page

Alternate path: In the event of an error,

1. System displays "error" dialog box

2. User pushes "continue" button

3. System returns to Action 2

Final state: Display

It also may be useful to use a spreadsheet or web form to gather the use case information in verbal format. Frequently, it is easiest to set up a spreadsheet template for the use cases, and to use the UML diagrams as ways to elicit requirements in workshops or to distribute them between the development and customer communities.

One way to find requirements that need to be clarified is to go back to the schedule estimates. Ask the implementation team which questions need to be answered for them to be able to provide a more accurate estimate. Sometimes the answers you get back will point at a major requirement that really needs to be nailed down.

Chapter 13 includes information on some tools that can be used to identify and communicate requirements.

INTERVIEWS TO GATHER REQUIREMENTS

The first step to gathering requirements is to identify who to interview. Generally speaking, the people closest to the business process in question are good people to answer questions about how the business process works.

Another good group of people to interview are the people who manage the application as it currently exists. They probably have a good view about what works and what does not in the current system.

Here are some questions that need to be answered to pull together requirements:

What benefits do we expect from this project?

What problems are we trying to solve?

Who will manage the system when it is complete?

Who are the direct users of the new system?

Who are the indirect customers for the new system?

Who does this system need to talk to? (Where does it get input from? Where does output go?)

What format constraints do we have on input and output?

What performance or Service Level Agreement (SLA) constraints exist for the system?

What sort of pain points exist with the current system?

Are there pain points adjacent to the existing system that can be eased by designing this system a little differently?

Are there training materials for the existing system that we can examine for requirements?

What do typical requests look like for the existing system? How are they currently processed?

Structuring Requirements

Requirements should be identified with a unique requirement number. Especially if there are more than a few requirements, it makes cross-referencing much easier when setting expectations for work packages or user acceptance testing.

It probably makes the most sense to structure requirements in a nested structure, with high-level requirements being broken down into lower-level requirements. See Example 4-2 for a simple example.

EXAMPLE 4-2: REQUIREMENT STRUCTURE

2.15: Obtain a database server

2.15.1: Server must be compatible with organization standards

2.15.2: Server must have at least 4 cores

2.15.3: Server must have at least 4 GB RAM

These numbers need to remain consistent throughout the project; you will drive yourself insane if you keep trying to update all the places a requirement number appears in the project documentation every time a requirement is removed or added. If a requirement is cancelled, the requirement document should be updated to reflect its cancellation, but the number should not be re-assigned.

Nonfunctional Requirements

In addition to describing the functioning of the system (functional requirements), there are a number of nonfunctional requirements that need to be considered. It may be necessary to negotiate some of these. Reaching certain thresholds, for example, may require a larger investment than the customer wanted. In that case, options can be presented as part of the scope conversation.

COMMON NONFUNCTIONAL REQUIREMENTS

Availability. Uptime and network availability requirements for different parts of the system.

Scalability. How quickly and easily additional resources can be brought online.

Portability. How easily the system can be moved. This may include moving it to a different platform or vendor.

Security. What type of security requirements are in place for the system or network communications.

Fault tolerance. How well the system deals with component failures.

Performance. How responsive the system is, and how much throughput capacity it has.

Usability. How user-friendly the system is.

Flexibility. How easy it is to bring additional features or components online.

Data integrity. The level of checking to ensure that data remains consistent and correct.

Acceptance Testing

Part of dealing with requirements is validating that they have been achieved in the final project result. If you specify what the requirements mean when you define them, it makes it much easier for the project team to hit them.

You will need to have representatives of the user community available to answer questions and to directly verify that the requirements have been met in user acceptance testing. The earlier components can be tested, the more time there will be to take care of any variances that appear.

Project Management Plan

The *project management plan* for each project will be unique. It needs to be complete, but should only include what is needed to complete the project successfully. This is a balance because a simple project will need a lot less detail and structure than a complex multiteam project.

Structure for a Project Management Plan

Depending on the environment where you find yourself, you may have a project management plan template that you are expected to use. Some common standards include templates that are included with Microsoft Project, as well as US Department of Defense standard 2167 and IEEE 1058-1998.

Here are some common sections and ideas that should be included in a project management plan:

- **Project name.** This should be a unique project name that can be used to help management track progress of this project.

- **Project description.** A brief description of the project in common language. It should include information on what the project is for, how much it will cost, and how long it will take.

- **Project sponsor.** The name and contact information for the sponsor of the project.

- **Project management team.** The names, positions, and contact information for the project managers and key stakeholder representatives. This should include a brief label indicating the role of each representative in the project.

- **Deliverables.** This section will be similar to what is in the project scope and should include pointers to more detailed documents as needed.

- **References.** Links to key reference or historical documents should be included. This may include references to organization processes, procedures, or policies that are relevant to the project.

- **Definitions.** Because this will be viewed by nontechnical people, the plan should have as little jargon as possible. Where jargon or technical terms are needed, they should be defined for nontechnical readers.

- **Organizational information.** This may include something like organizational charts for the people working on the project, as well as a description of the roles of the different people involved in the project.

- **Management objectives.** Management's view of the project's priorities and constraints.

- **Controls.** Description of how the project progress will be tracked, how changes will be authorized, and any gates or milestone approvals that will be used during the project's lifetime.

- **Risk management.** How the project team will identify, report, and track risks and issues identified during the project.

- **Staffing.** Which type of experts are needed to execute the project, and from which groups?

- **Tools and processes.** What tools will be used to document and track the project and its deliverables? How will the information be recorded using these tools?

- **Work breakdown structure (WBS).**

- **Deliverables.** Similar to what is in the scope document, including information about quality expectations.

- **Schedule.** For anything beyond the trivial, both a summary and a detailed schedule should be provided. If the WBS is built properly, that can help build the schedule.

- **Budget.** Both a summary and a detailed budget should be specified.

Risk Management

The project manager should get agreement to a *risk management plan* as part of the initial project plan approval. This includes maintaining a register of risks and issues associated with the project.

Some elements to include in a risk management plan are the following:

- **Contingency plans** for risks that are foreseen early in the project.

- **Fallback plans** for risks that may have an especially significant impact on project delivery.

- **Contingency reserves** of time, money, resources, or approvals that can be accessed by the project management team to deal with risks.

Note One way to rank risks is to express the likelihood as a percentage, and the impact in dollars. (This may mean translating project delays or man hours into a rough dollar figure.) Multiply those numbers for each risk, and compare the results to rank which risks need the most urgent attention.

For example, if risk A has a 50% likelihood of costing $10,000, and risk B has a 10% likelihood of costing $20,000, then risk A has an expected cost of $5,000 (.50 × $10,000), and risk B has an expected cost of $2,000 (.10 × $20,000). Risk A would be considered the more urgent risk, in this case.

Risk Responses

Risks can be dealt with in one of the following ways:

- **Avoidance.** The threat is entirely avoided, probably by eliminating the causes.

- **Mitigation.** This means that the risk is reduced to acceptable levels by taking an action or setting up a contingency plan.

- **Transference.** The negative effects of the risk are assumed by another party. Insurance is a good example of risk transference.

- **Acceptance.** The risk's downside and likelihood can be examined to see if the organization is willing to accept the risk. Usually, this will only be the case if mitigation actions have been taken to reduce the risk to acceptable levels.

Tracking Risks

Risks need to be tracked by the project management team. A *risk register* should be published and made available to the stakeholder community. Project team members should report all known risks to the register to be analyzed, and the project management team should set up interviews and brainstorming sessions early in the planning process to try to identify known risks.

ELEMENTS OF ENTRIES IN THE RISKS AND ISSUES REGISTER

Unique identifier. If a unique number is assigned to each risk, it makes it easier to cross-reference the risk in other project documents.

Seriousness. The seriousness of the risk should be ranked, perhaps with a numerical scale indicating how serious the risk has been evaluated to be, based on its likelihood and potential impact.

Name. The risk should be given a unique short descriptive name for discussion.

Description. The risk should be described, or a document containing a full description can be referenced.

Category. This will indicate which part of the project team needs to deal with the risk or its impact.

Root cause. Chapter 9 discusses how to perform a root cause analysis, if needed for this risk.

Triggers. Symptoms that indicate that the risk may be active.

Responses. Mitigation actions, contingency plans, or other possible responses to the risk.

Owner. The person assigned to deal with the risk.

Likelihood. How likely is the risk to occur? This could be in percentages, or in terms of high/medium/low.

Impact. What is the downside risk?

Status. Has the risk been mitigated or accepted?

Dependency Management

As the project progresses, the project manager is responsible for looking at how the dependency relationships are affecting the overall project timeline. In particular, the project manager needs to keep a close eye on the sequence of tasks that make up the critical path.

A *dependency* is a relationship between tasks that has an impact on how they are sequenced or scheduled.

- **Mandatory.** Some dependencies are inherent in the nature of the tasks. These are known as *mandatory dependencies*. You can't install a database until the server is powered up, for example.

- **Discretionary.** These are driven by the project management team or by the practices and procedures in place in the environment. For example, you don't want to start coding until the requirements are defined.

- **External.** Some dependencies are driven by items external to the project. These should be tracked on the WBS, along with expected delivery dates.

There are a few different ways that dependency relationships can have an impact on task scheduling. It is important to track the type of dependency, as these can have very different effects on scheduling.

- **Finish to start.** The first task must completed before the second task can begin.

- **Start to start.** The second task cannot start until the first task does.

- **Finish to finish.** The second task cannot finish until the first task does.

- **Start to finish.** The second task cannot finish until the first task starts.

There are several ways to diagram dependencies. Project management software, such as Microsoft Project and GanttProject, will take care of these diagrams for you, as long as you put the dependency information into the project plan. In general, dependency relationships are represented on a network diagram, where the first task is at the tail of an arrow, and the second task is at the point. Depending on the type of network diagram and type of dependency, the arrow location and shape may be different.

Interface Management

The points of interaction between the groups and elements of the project are a particular type of dependency that needs special attention.

When these interfaces are points of contact between two groups, you are responsible for making sure that they are working together smoothly and communicating the information needed so that their respective contributions come together correctly.

The number of interfaces grows very quickly as the number of elements increases. A good project manager is able to identify the critical interfaces early and monitor them throughout the project cycle. When these interfaces break down, that will affect multiple elements of the project plan.

Milestones

There are certain places in the project plan that are natural places for making sure that the project is remaining on track. These milestones need to be tracked to make sure that the overall project is remaining on schedule. They also should be reported to the stakeholder community to build confidence in the project and a sense of momentum that will help carry the project through to completion.

Milestones need to be specific, measurable, assignable, realistic, and time framed. (Project managers refer to these as *SMART milestones.*) Beyond that, they need to be well-chosen, to reflect the progress of major phases of the overall project.

Staying on Track

The time estimates in the WBS are an important tool for tracking whether you are on target to hit a milestone. Items on the critical path are the ones that need the most focus, but the critical path may shift as people report different work packages completed or delayed. Make sure to get status on each work package, including time estimates.

Publish the time estimates provided by the project team. If the estimates are not written down and tracked, they will slide. When things are delayed, as they will be, work with the accountable people to find out why and try to identify a way to get the project plan back on track.

Periodic Reviews

Milestones are also appropriate times to review project progress. In the event that the cost and/or schedule are increasing rapidly, these reviews are the time to either adjust the scope, commit the additional resources, or maybe even scrap the project.

These reviews are sometimes referred to as "kill points." The worst thing to happen to a project is to have its costs spiral out of control, and never to produce anything. If the project starts to go down that path, it may be best to kill it and go back to the "concept" phase to replan.

Each project phase should be considered to be a milestone. At each phase of the project, the project manager is responsible for checking with stakeholders for agreement that the project is meeting the project requirements.

Identify and Schedule Resources

As different resources will be needed during the project execution, the project manager is responsible for lining them up. This includes people as well as facilities, equipment, or vendor participation.

One of the most important duties of a project manager is to look around the corner to see the next approaching pain point, and to arrange to alleviate it before anybody else realizes it is coming.

Stay in touch with the people who are executing the work, and provide opportunities for them to approach you with problems. These problems can have downstream effects on resource requirements and scheduling for other parts of the project.

Scope Change Control

Scope and requirement changes are sometimes necessary, but they are costly in both money and time. Changes should not be undertaken lightly. The project manager is responsible for making sure that any changes to scope or requirements have complete buy-in, including explicit commitments of the resources needed to implement the changes.

Part of a project manager's job is tracking these changes and considering their impact on other parts of the project. The project as a whole may be delayed as a result of a change to a particular component or task.

During the project, the project manager will need to identify, evaluate, and manage the changes that are proposed during the project. Team members need to understand that changes need to go through the approval process; otherwise time will be wasted with intergroup conflict, and it may be necessary to destroy something that was close to completion if it includes unauthorized changes.

Changes can be the most contentious part of a project. Project managers need to be well-organized and retain documentation about changes that are considered, rejected, accepted, and implemented. Documents to be tracked include:

- Change requests, and whether they are approved or rejected.
- Reported defects, either in the plan or in the product.
- Remediation actions taken to resolve these defects.
- Preventative actions taken to avoid issues.
- Approved updates to the project scope and plan.

It is unwieldy to get approval from every stakeholder for every change. Most changes would be reviewed and approved by a change control board (CCB) made up of representatives of the key stakeholder groups. It usually makes sense to have regularly scheduled CCB meetings so that team members know when changes need to be submitted, and when an answer can be expected. In a time-sensitive project, CCB review meetings should be scheduled frequently.

The CCB needs to include enough representation from the key communities to ensure that risk assessments and necessary communications have been carried out properly. The project management team, user community representatives, stakeholder representatives, engineering and development resources, and other specialty communities should be represented on the CCB.

Team members also will need guidance on the format that is expected for change requests.

Reporting Project Status

Execution is great, but the plug will be pulled on the project unless the project sponsor and the key stakeholders are able to see concrete progress. It is the project manager's responsibility to provide accurate reports of the project status.

You will want to develop standard templates or a dashboard for reporting project status. The goal is to allow stakeholders to identify project status at a glance, preferably without interrupting you for a personalized update.

When a Project Is in Trouble

Killing a project is a huge decision, especially if a project has been allowed to meander out of control for some time. Being the project manager for a large failed project is a career limiting move. If you keep tight control from the outset, you are much less likely to have to kill a project further along.

The crisis moment when people decide to kill a project is almost never the first sign of trouble. Trouble should have appeared earlier, when someone realized that the dependency relationships were wrong, or the amount of time for a task was totally wrong, or that something happened that was going to blow out the budget. When things go wrong, they will not fix themselves. Jump in right away to get the project back on a firm footing.

- **Convene a meeting of the technical experts to find out what the situation is.** Make sure everyone understands the difficulty. Collect ideas on how the difficulty can be worked around.

- **Collect all the information, but get it quickly.** You do not have time for analysis paralysis.

- **Present the difficulty and any needed changes to the project sponsor.** Changes will need to be approved by the stakeholders.

- **Reward people who bring problems into the light.** "Shoot the messenger" reactions just mean that you won't find out about the next problem in time to do anything about it.

- **After the difficulty is resolved, convene a "lessons learned" session to identify what went wrong in the planning process.** Might the same thing have happened in another part of the project plan? If so, fix it now.

Most people are reluctant to come forward and say that a project is in trouble. One way of identifying projects that are in trouble is known as *earned value management* (EVM).

Earned Value Management

EVM is a method for tracking the costs of a project and making sure that the money spent on the project is being matched by progress on the project. EVM involves calculating the following:

- **Planned value (PV).** This is the amount of money budgeted to be spent during a project period. "PV to date" refers to the total planned value expected to have been spent on the project to this point in time.

- **Actual cost (AC).** This is the amount actually spent during that time.

- **Budgeted actual cost (BAC).** This is the amount that is budgeted for the entire project.

- **Earned value (EV).** This is an estimate of the value of the work completed during the time period.

- **Rate of performance (RP).** This is the fraction of planned work that was to have been completed by the end of the time period. (This can be calculated based on the percentage completion numbers from the WBS.)

- **Cost variance (CV).** This is a comparison of the amount expected to have been spent during a time period against the amount actually spent. It reflects whether the work costs more or less than expected, based on whether the CV is negative or positive, respectively.

- **Schedule variance (SV).** Similar to CV, this reflects the amount of work completed against the amount of work expected to have been completed.

- **Cost performance index (CPI).** This is a measure of how well the project is staying within its cost estimates.

- **Schedule performance index (SPI).** This is a measure of how well the project is staying within its schedule estimates.

- **Estimated actual cost (EAC).** This is the estimate of what will actually be spent, assuming that the CPI remains constant through the rest of the project.

- **Estimated time to complete (ETC).** This is an estimate of the amount of time that will be needed for the overall project, assuming that the SPI remains constant through the rest of the project.

The following are the formulas used to calculate the variances using the EVM.

- EV = (PV to date) × RP
- CV = EV − AC
- SV = EV − PV
- CPI = EV/AC
- SPI = EV/PV
- EAC = BAC/CPI
- ETC = (original time estimate)/SPI

EXAMPLE 4-3: EXAMPLE EVM CALCULATION

Assume that the amount expected to have been spent to date is $10,000, that the actual amount spent was $15,000, and that the percentage of planned work completed so far is 50%.

EV = $10,000 × 0.50 = $5,000

CV = $5,000 − $15,000 = −$10,000

SV = $5,000 − $10,000 = −$5,000

CPI = $5,000/$15,000 = 0.33

SPI = $5,000/$10,000 = 0.5

The key numbers are:

EAC = BAC/.33 = BAC × 3 (i.e., the cost is expected to come in three times as high as budgeted.)

ETC = (original time estimate)/.5 = (original time estimate) × 2 (i.e., the time is expected to come in as twice as long as originally estimated.)

Example 4-3 shows EVM calculations for a project that is running over budget and behind schedule. If someone told you that the project was going slower than expected and still running over its budget, you would know that the project was in trouble. EVM gives you a quantitative tool to estimate just how bad the damage is, and to compare projects that are in trouble.

Quality Management

To deliver a quality product at the end of the project, you have to track the quality of the deliverables throughout. This will involve having a test plan in place that will validate the different deliverables as they are reported complete.

Beyond checking the quality of the deliverables, you also have to check that the interfaces between different components work properly.

Most important of all, you have to verify that the project meets the requirements of the user community. This is best checked as thoroughly as possible while the project is running, rather than delivering a complete package at the end for verification. To the extent that prototyping and test harnesses can be used to allow users to check components, you will be able to avoid unpleasant surprises at project delivery time.

A high-quality project deliverable will both conform with the requirements for that deliverable, and will also be fit for use in the manner intended. If both things are not true, the quality of the deliverable is not acceptable.

To have high quality, you need your planning process to support good requirements gathering, your quality assurance process needs to guarantee that deliverables are of acceptable quality, and your quality control process needs to identify and implement ways to improve quality.

Quality is usually measured by testing. If the detailed requirements are complete, the test plan can follow what is specified for each requirement. Each requirement should include one or more acceptance tests for determining whether the requirement was met.

Some important criteria for acceptance tests are:

- **Functionality.** Does the component meet its functional requirements?

- **Outputs.** Are the outputs from the component produced in the required format? This is important whether the output is intended for a user interface or a program interface.

- **Performance.** Is the performance and system resource utilization of the component adequate for real-world operation?

- **Reliability.** How maintainable and reliable is the component?

Testing needs to be performed at several different levels as project components are delivered. These can be combined to the extent practical, in order not to leave rework or major problems to be discovered at the last possible moment.

- **Code review.** Any code should go through a review process. It needs to comply with naming, structure, and documentation standards for the organization.

- **Unit test.** Each component is tested by itself, perhaps in a test harness, to ensure that it fulfills its requirements.

- **Integration test.** Each component is tested in combination with the components that share an interface with it.

- **System test.** The complete system is tested by the implementation team.

- **User acceptance test.** The complete system is tested by representatives of the user community.

The earlier in the process an error is caught, the less expensive it will be to fix it. The amount of time saved by an appropriate review and testing schedule will more than pay for itself over the course of the project.

Reviews are critical. It is impossible to simply "test in" good quality. Good quality starts with good requirements and a good design, then continues through the rest of the build process. Good quality is built in from the ground up.

When management decides to cut time from the project, testing is usually the first target. That is a false sense of savings; the time cut from the project plan is likely to be more than wasted in dealing with the problems that were not caught earlier in the process.

Sometimes problems emerge in testing that need to be identified. Chapter 9 discusses tools that can be used in group troubleshooting and root cause analysis sessions.

Project Delivery

When the project is delivered, the project manager's job is not done yet. There are still a few more tasks that should be undertaken to wrap up the project.

- **User acceptance results.** Document the user community's sign-off that project requirements have been met.

- **Lessons learned.** Obtain information from the project team about lessons that have been learned during the project's execution.

- **Finalize project documentation.** Finish filling out the WBS with delivery times, and archive project documentation for reference by the next project manager.

- **Final budget.** Prepare the final project financial statements, including expected maintenance and other costs during the expected lifetime of the project's deliverables.

Summary

Project management is a discipline that every IT leader should study. It provides a structured, standard way to organize projects. Your organization can benefit from the discipline to use a standard project management process.

Discussion Questions

Think of a project you have been involved in.

1. Which factors lead to its success or failure?

2. How could things have been organized differently to increase the success of the project?

3. Does your organization have a project management process in place? What could be done to improve it?

4. What types of projects would benefit from an iterative development model?

Further Reading

Berkun, Scott. *Making Things Happen*. Sebastopol, CA: O'Reilly, 2008.

Braude, Eric J. *Software Engineering: An Object-Oriented Perspective*. Danvers, MA: Wiley, 2001.

Schwalbe, Kathy. *Information Technology Project Management*. Boston, MA: Thompson, 2006.

Stellman, Andrew, and Jennifer Greene. *Applied Software Project Management*. Sebastopol, CA: O'Reilly, 2006.

Documenting Policies and Procedures

During your initial 90 days, one of the things you need to look at is how your team's processes and procedures are documented.

To the extent that you can use standard, documented processes, costly errors will be avoided. Not only does that make the environment more stable, it improves the quality of life of your staff, especially your senior staff.

Your documentation should be easy to find, edit, and update. There are a number of possible ways of doing this, including file shares, wiki or blog pages, and SharePoint. If there is an organization-wide standard, it makes sense to support it.

Documentation should be produced for both internal team use and for people outside of the team.

The documentation for people outside of the team should focus on what services the team can provide, and how requests should be filed and formatted. People should be instructed how to open a ticket, and they should be told what type of information and approvals are required for what types of requests. (If budget approval is required, that should be included in the request as well.)

If people know what information they have to provide for your team to fulfill the request sooner, it will help both the requester and the person from your team who executes the request.

Your documentation repository should include some type of index to make it easier to find documents (and to avoid creating duplicates). It should also include links out to other teams' documentation or to organizational standards that need to be followed.

It is possible to go crazy with documentation. The bottom line is the bottom line, and you will be judged by the functionality and reliability of the environment you are responsible for. Documentation is a tool to help you make the environment more stable and more flexible. Start with the documentation tasks that will help you achieve these goals, and work to build a culture where documentation is part of every deployment and every change.

POLICIES, STANDARDS, PROCESSES, AND PROCEDURES

Policies are statements by management that provide requirements to guide the people who implement technologies and processes.

Standards are organization-wide platforms and methods that support the policies.

Processes are business methods and practices that support the standards.

Procedures are step-by-step instructions on how to carry out a task in a way that supports the organization's policies and standards.

Procedures

Ideally, every task would have a specific, standard procedure that has been vetted and approved as complying with policy. That is the ideal, but it is a very tall order.

In the real world, your group probably has some well-defined procedures, some procedures that have only recently been drafted, some procedures that exist only as emails or comments in a script, and some procedures that are so out of date that they would break the environment if someone actually tried to carry them out.

Some of your early wins should come from identifying the biggest gaps in your documented procedures and filling those gaps. Focus your attention first on procedures that:

- Are frequently executed.
- Have a similar procedure each time they are executed.
- Are able to be executed by more junior team members.
- Are related to security or audit concerns (e.g., access-related requests or patch installation procedures).

In particular, if it is a procedure that will be entered into change control requests or audit responses over and over, it is far better to have a standard document that can just be attached (or a link that can be provided).

You may need to work to get policies approved, if you see a gap in the policy structure. At the technology team level, your focus will probably be on procedures and maybe standards. Policies and standards are discussed in greater detail in the final two sections of this chapter.

Procedures as Controls

When management defines a policy, they expect that the organization will comply with it. The enforcement of these policies is only possible if we track and verify compliance and report breaches of the policy.

A *control* is a method or facility that is used to enforce a policy. Procedures that implement a policy are examples of controls. Compliance teams may call on technology teams to certify that the procedures are documented, and that they are in active use.

Demonstrating compliance can be done by logging changes, along with the procedures used. If the procedure can be automated, it becomes even easier to demonstrate compliance, especially if the automated procedure includes a logging step.

Changes that are controlled by a policy should be tracked and logged. If you have a working ticketing system, it is easier to require that the requests be filed as tickets in a standard format. Then the person fulfilling the request can update the ticket with the procedure used when the ticket is marked as resolved.

When new facilities are added, controls should be built into the system at implementation time. The initial requirements should include implementing the controls. Because new implementations should be tested anyway, the testing procedures may serve double duty as compliance controls.

Automation

While looking for procedures that are priorities for documentation, keep an eye out for simple tasks that are done frequently. To the extent possible, these should be automated and even made into self-service requests for the customer.

Another target for automation would be multistep procedures that are not done frequently enough for people to be able to remember all the steps. If these can be scripted and documented, it will make a big difference in the reliability of the environment.

You will never be given enough staff or enough time to carry out the full extent of your duties. The way to work around this is to identify time-consuming tasks or frequent tasks that can be automated. It takes some extra effort to develop, review, test, and deploy automated processes, but the time saved can be rolled into the next automation project. If you pick the right targets, automation projects can be good sources of early wins when you take over an environment.

Change Control

Uncontrolled change is the enemy of a reliable environment. There are several important components of a functional change management system:

- A system for obtaining approvals from stakeholders for changes.

- A system for tracking change requests through the review and approval process.

- A process for reviewing change requests.

- Each change needs to include a brief description of the change, a specific plan of how the change will be executed, a specific plan for backing out the change, and the success criteria that will be used to test the change.

Each change should pass through several phases on its way to implementation:

- **Assessment.** The risks of implementing the change need to be considered. Part of the assessment is testing the change and the back-out plans beforehand.

- **Planning.** A procedure needs to be created and reviewed for executing the change, testing it, and backing out if necessary.

- **Testing.** The procedure should be tested. How it is tested will depend on the nature of the change. If the procedure is standard, additional testing may not be necessary. If like-for-like testing is impossible, the procedure needs to be reviewed by the relevant subject-matter experts.

- **Communication.** The change needs to be communicated to all of the stakeholders, including the information about what the change is, what the expected impact is, why it is necessary, and when it will be executed. The time, format, and manner of these notifications should be standardized, so people know where and when to look for them.

- **Authorization.** The appropriate customer or service owner needs to approve the change, based on the information from the procedure and the assessment.

- **Documentation.** The change needs to be thoroughly documented in a standard manner and location. Each change record should include information on the requester, approver, system status before the change, reason for the change, specifics of the change, status after the change, whether the change was successful, whether the back-out was successful (if the change failed), dates and times of the different elements, and contact information for the implementer.

- **Validation.** The requester and/or end-user community needs to validate the system after the change and provide a certification that the change was successful.

  Part of making the change control system work properly is that you need people in different roles to review and approve changes:

- **Change requester.** This may be an internal customer, or it could be someone from the technical staff. The change requester specifies the requirements and scope of the change.

- **Change owner.** This is the person who shepherds the change request through the change control process.

- **Change implementer.** This is the person who is responsible for implementing the change.

Incident Response

An incident is something that occurs outside of the normal functioning of the environment. Some incidents may result in a production service being affected in a measurable way. Depending on the nature of the impact, it may be necessary to execute an emergency change.

A typical incident will flow through the following phases, illustrated by Figure 5-1:

Detection   Classification   Investigation   Resolution   Closure

Figure 5-1. Incident Response

- **Detection and recording.** Ideally, the monitoring system should open a ticket directly into the correct queue.

- **Classification and initial response.** Someone from the team owning that queue verifies whether there is a legitimate incident, and does a preliminary investigation into the scope and cause of the problem.

- **Investigation and diagnosis.** The relevant technical teams perform a more thorough investigation to diagnose the problem and propose a resolution.

- **Resolution and recovery.** The resolution is implemented and the service recovered.

- **Incident closure.** The incident is closed, and the customer representative validates the service.

The incident response framework needs to consider some important elements of incident response: ownership, monitoring, tracking, and communication.

WHEN YOU DON'T HAVE TIME TO ASK PERMISSION

Sometimes there is not time to get proper authorization for a change in advance. If there is an outage or other emergency, it may be necessary to change things on the fly to restore service. There are a few principles to keep in mind when you find yourself in this situation:

- Don't do anything that can't be reversed.

- Keep track of everything you do.

- Follow the organization's incident response process.

- Report on the changes you introduced into the environment after the fact.

- Those changes should be reviewed once the emergency is past. If the review board decides to keep them, they can stay as part of an emergency change. Otherwise, they can be reverted as part of a scheduled change.

Don't hide the actions you take to resolve a problem. Report them honestly and help clean up and document the environment as needed.

Incident response should be handled in a standard way to instruct and protect the operations and implementation teams. Here are some common elements that need to be defined:

- Time frame for the response as frequently defined in the Service Level Agreement (SLA) for the facility in question.

- Notification requirements for the response and stakeholder teams.

- How problem resolutions should be tracked, logged, and approved.

- How logs and other evidence should be preserved.

- Process for analyzing logs, documentation, and other evidence to perform a root cause analysis.

- Change control process for implementing necessary changes or for approving emergency changes.

Outages need to be tracked, including impact to service levels, the outcome of the root cause analysis, and the actions taken to resolve the outage. Outage reports should be stored in a standard format and location so they can be reviewed to look for patterns on how to improve the reliability of the environment.

Policy Approvals

Because policies bind the organization, they need to be approved at a level that will be recognized.

A lot of organizations have to provide evidence of compliance with policies as part of audits. This involves setting up controls and investments of capital and staff time to maintain the controls. Because most organizations have regulatory and contractual requirements that they have to comply with anyway, it makes sense to have policies that reinforce compliance.

There are several constituent groups within the organization that need to approve a policy for it to take effect.

- Depending on the nature of the policy, the legal or compliance department may need to review the proposed policy to make sure it meets regulatory or contractual requirements.

- The architecture team needs to review the policy and possibly raise flags about costs required to change the technology landscape to make compliance possible.

- The technology teams who would implement the policy need to review it to raise flags about additional costs or requirements that will be needed to support the policy.

- Management needs to review the policy to decide if it represents a business priority, and if the proposed policy reflects the organization's goals.

The approvals for a policy need to happen at a sufficiently high managerial level that the policy's legitimacy will be recognized by all the relevant teams.

Once a policy is approved, it needs to be published. Organizations should have a standard way to store, approve, and communicate policies. If policies are not published in a standard location, people will not be able to refer to them to comply with them.

Policies are supported by standards and procedures. Part of the approval process for a policy has to include drafting and approvals of these standards and procedures. But there is no need to have those standards and procedures approved by upper management.

In some cases, it may be appropriate to refer a new standard or procedure to the compliance team, but the technology architecture and implementation teams usually control things at that level. Just as most technology people are not lawyers, most lawyers are not competent to judge technology.

Standards

Sometimes technologists see standards as confining. When an enterprise standard exists, sometimes that means that the absolute optimal solution for a particular problem cannot be found.

Ideally, standards should be liberating. If there is a standard way to roll out large parts of the technology infrastructure, it will help the operations teams maintain the technology, as it reduces the number of platform issues that need to be tracked and resolved. It will help the development teams because templates and code libraries are able to be re-used. And it will produce a better overall environment because standards promote more efficient, reliable functioning of the environment.

Summary

Documentation is the key to mature, effective, repeatable processes. Effective procedures are documented, followed, and updated. Learning to manage documentation effectively will be a key to your long-term success as a manager.

Discussion Questions

1. Effective policies are clear and definite. Write a policy for something in your environment that you know well. What was the hardest part of writing that policy?

2. Examine a procedure document you produced in the past. If you did not understand the procedure well, would you be able to follow the document? How frequently should this document be updated?

Further Reading

Greene, Sari Stern. *Security Policies and Procedures: Principles and Practices*. Upper Saddle River, NJ: Pearson, 2006.

Harvard Business Essentials. *Manager's Toolkit*. Boston, MA: Harvard Business School Press, 2004.

Peltier, Thomas R. *Information Security Policies and Procedures*. Boca Raton, FL: Auerbach, 2004.

Building Your Team

In Chapter 2, we discussed the importance of assessing the people on your team early in your tenure. Your team members can be characterized in one of the following ways:

- **Key player.** Keep these people where they are.

- **Development project.** This person isn't quite there, but shows potential. Work out a plan to develop it.

- **Move.** This person might fit better in a different role.

- **Observe.** You aren't going to figure out everyone right away. Give yourself space to watch and think if you aren't sure.

- **Replace eventually.** This person should be replaced, but it can be done at the right time.

- **Replace immediately.** Find a way to move this person out. This can either be someone who has an attitude problem that can't be resolved, or someone who is irredeemably incompetent.

In your evaluation, look at more than the technical competence of the person in question. Sometimes a person is contributing more to the team than you see at first glance. Include things like the energy the person brings to the team, the judgment shown during team meetings, or the relationships the person has with other peer groups. Also make sure to think about whether you can trust that person to help you implement the changes you need.

By the end of the 90 days, you have had plenty of time to observe your team in action. You should know who is staying, who is going, and who is moving. Communicate that information to your boss, and eventually to the other key stakeholders. By the end of 6 months, you should have the people in place that you need to run your team.

The difficulty is that some of the people to be replaced have critical knowledge and skills. You need to identify a plan for doing this with as little disruption as possible. Temporary help can be hired during the transition, or maybe a more junior person is ready to step into the opening. In any case, a plan needs to be approved and implemented.

Recruiting the Right People

Recruiting is expensive, so you need to make sure to do it the right way. Understand which qualifications are actually necessary, and which are nice to have. Take into account the skill profile of the other team members, so that you know where you can compromise and where you can't.

Also take into account how the team members would work together. Try to assemble a group of people whose strengths are complementary, and who will work together well.

Hold out for high-character applicants. Hiring the wrong person is expensive in both time and money.

Reassure the people you want to keep. When good people see churn in the team, they may start looking at other opportunities themselves. Speak to HR about the constraints you have on what you can and cannot say. There are ways to signal your appreciation to people you want to keep without crossing any legal or ethical boundaries.

When you post a job opening, you need to identify what the requirements for the job actually are:

- Primary and secondary responsibilities for the role.
- Education and experience required.
- Personal characteristics and skills (e.g., strong organizational skills, able to work independently)
- A personality match with the team and organizational culture and with your managerial style. (Note that issues in this category cannot be used to discriminate against several protected classes.)

A job posting is a good chance to rethink what that position should be, as opposed to what the former employee's characteristics were. Maybe it makes more sense to shift responsibilities differently within the team and to redefine the role.

> **Note** If you can hire someone with industry or business experience that can also be a big benefit. Every industry has its own rhythm, and it helps to get someone who already understands the unspoken expectations. And when it comes time to gather requirements, someone who understands the business has a huge advantage.

Once you have the requirements in mind, you can write up a job description. This will need to be vetted by HR to verify that you are not impinging on any legal requirements.

- Job title.

- Organization and business unit name.

- Hiring and reporting managers (identify both, if they are not the same).

- Responsibilities.

- Compensation.

- Expected work schedule and location.

- Educational and experience requirements. Distinguish between hard requirements and "nice to haves."

- Personal requirements.

A lot of technical people can't write a well-structured résumé to save themselves. I have found some gems by being a little forgiving on the résumé and depending on a phone screening to weed out people whose résumé reflects more experience than the candidate actually has. It depends on the nature of the team and the opening you are trying to fill.

> **Note** A well-written résumé is definitely a good indicator to look for. The ability to express yourself well in writing in a business context is a terrific qualification. Most technical teams have a shortage of people who can communicate well with the business side.

RÉSUMÉ RED FLAGS

There are some things to watch out for when reviewing résumés:

Emphasis on education and training classes over experience. This may indicate a weakness in real-world experience.

Gaps in service or lots of short-term jobs. This may just indicate someone who has been doing consulting, but you need to find out.

Either too much or not enough variety in job descriptions between different positions. I've spoken with several candidates who seem to have repeated the same one year of experience five or eight times.

Descriptions of positions, with no descriptions of interesting projects or accomplishments.

My preference is to make notes on résumés listing topics I want to investigate further (based on red flags I see). Then I set up short phone screenings. Based on the phone screenings, I call back a small number for in-person interviews, and hire from there after checking references.

You want to make sure that all applicants respond to a core set of questions so you can make fair comparisons without being prejudiced either for or against a candidate. In addition to the core questions, ask questions raised by oddities in their résumé, and let the candidate speak about his or her strengths.

The interviewer needs to keep control of the pace of the interview. Some candidates are particularly good at snowing interviewers. They entertain the interviewer and avoid the tough questions by playing out the clock.

No more than 10% of the interview time should be taken by a brief, scripted introduction to the organization and what the position entails. If there is a serious, potentially disqualifying question that needs to be asked, ask it up front. Then roll into your core interview questions. Finally, finish up with other questions. It is your responsibility to keep control of the pace of the interview.

There are a number of questions that cannot be asked, such as questions about race, ethnicity, sexual preference, family situation, health conditions, age, weight, or religion. Your HR department should be able to provide guidance about questions to avoid. They also may want to review your core set of questions.

Leave time for the interviewee to speak about what makes him or her the ideal candidate for the job. Sometimes that can be the most interesting part of the interview.

▓ **Note** If you can get the candidates to tell you stories about their proudest accomplishments, you can learn a lot. Listen to how they speak about their roles in projects they worked on. Did they lead? Or just follow instructions? Drill down on special accomplishments to make sure that they are not reflecting someone else's victory.

Leave about 10% of the interview time at the end to wrap up and allow the candidate to ask questions about the position. Shake hands, make eye contact, and walk the candidate out.

At the end, write down notes about your impressions. When there is a long time between interviews, or when there are a lot of interviews together, it is easy to get impressions confused between interviewees. You can use your notes to keep people straight.

Check references when you are close to a decision, before you extend an offer. Most people who have been around IT for a while know horror stories about people who can talk a much better game than they can execute. Reference checks are one of the few safeguards you have against this problem.

Team Formation

Bruce Tuckman developed a model of team formation in the 1960s and 1970s.[1] The stages he described seem ubiquitous to team formations in different circumstances:

- **Forming.** New team members are introduced, and people learn about each other.
- **Storming.** Conflicts emerge between different ways of doing things.
- **Norming.** Team members develop ways of cooperating and working together.
- **Performing.** Team members have developed trust and understanding, and are able to work together effectively.
- **Adjourning.** The team breaks up.

Some amount of conflict is inevitable when people start working together. The team's leader should understand that this is natural, but should work to accelerate the development of ways for team members to work together productively.

Pay particular attention to people who are in different geographic locations, and especially in different time zones. You need to schedule extra time to interact with them and to draw them into the team dynamic. Geographic and time differences will slow down their interaction with the rest of the team, and will delay their ability to move into the norming and performing stages. You can't afford to lose part of your team like this; make a conscious effort to draw them in and keep them involved.

Large teams also can slow down the norming process because there are more interpersonal connections for the storming phase to operate over. You can

[1]Bruce Tuckman, "Developmental Sequence in Small Groups," *Psychological Bulletin* 63, no. 6 (1965): 384–99.

work around this to some extent by breaking the larger team into work groups of three to seven.

In some cases, team-building activities can help. In my experience, the best way to move from the storming to the norming phase is to go after some early wins. Shared success builds team working relationships faster than anything else I know.

Goals

A goal-setting exercise allows you to work one-on-one with your direct report to identify specific ways he or she can help the company move forward. It is usually ineffective for a manager to specify goals, and it is almost meaningless if the employee sets goals without input. A functional goal-setting process will involve input from both the employee and the manager.

To be effective, goals need to be

- Easily understood.

- Written down in a permanent location.

- Specific in criteria and time.

- Challenging but achievable.

- Recognized as important and aligned with the organizational strategy.

If a goal's objectives are not measurable, the goal becomes meaningless. The specific goal needs to have a specific measurement associated with success. "Learn Java" is not measurable. "Pass the Java exam with a score of 80% or higher" is.

As a manager, you should mentor your direct reports on how to meet their goals, once you have agreed on a set of important, measurable, and specific goals. Each goal should be broken into tasks, each of which will have a timeline. As a manager, it is your job to ensure that the employee has the resources necessary to execute the agreed-on plan.

Your job does not stop there. You need to review each employee's progress toward their goals periodically, and you will need to write up their employee review for their file with the outcome of the goals at the end of the review period.

Motivation

Different employees are motivated differently.

Money is important, of course. Compensation is a raw measure of how much someone is valued by the employer; make sure your people are fairly compensated or you will lose them.

Beyond monetary compensation, there are a lot of other incentives you as a manager can use to help motivate your team members.

Incentives

Incentives may include money and bonuses. If they do, establish clear and objective criteria, even if these are not shared with team members. (You don't want them gaming the system.)

Technical professionals like to make things work, and they like to be part of a successful team. Provide growth opportunities, and recognize people within the team when they contribute.

Track each person's contributions to the team, and report on them regularly. Personalized year-end summaries of accomplishments for team members demonstrate that you really are paying attention to what they are contributing.

A "thank you" goes a long way. When someone from your team stays up late or works a weekend to resolve a problem, send them a detailed thank you email, and cc your boss.

Save those thank you emails in a folder for each employee. When annual review time rolls around, you'll have some specific accomplishments you can reference.

The main reasons people will stay in a job are:[2]

- Pride in contributing to a respected organization.
- Respect for an immediate supervisor.
- Fair market-rate compensation. This can include intangible compensation, such as opportunities to learn new technologies.
- Friendships and respect for colleagues.
- Meaningful, challenging work.

---

[2]Harvard Business Essentials. *Manager's Toolkit*. Boston, MA: Harvard Business School Press, 2004.

The main reasons people leave are:

- Shift in organizational leadership.
- Conflict with an immediate supervisor.
- Friends leave.
- Shifts in responsibilities to something less desirable.
- Unfavorable work-life balance.

Money is important, but there are a lot of intangible things that you can use to help retain employees. Most of all, try not to be a jerk. You don't have to be a buddy; you just have to be fair and reasonable. Here are some things you can do to improve retention without hitting the bottom line:

- **Start people off right.** Make sure to get them up and running as quickly as possible. This means some prep work on your part before the employee arrives. If you can get them through orientation, and get their computer, phone, and email working right away, it will make a big difference to the new employee's mindset about your organization and your team.

- **Be demanding but fair.** People expect to come to work to get things done. Be explicit about your expectations, and make sure that the expectations are reasonable.

- **Share information.** People like to understand how their efforts contribute to the larger whole.

- **Give people autonomy.** Set expectations, follow up to check status, but don't micromanage.

- **Give your employees a chance to stretch.** Good employees like to accomplish new and challenging things. If you can't find something challenging for them to accomplish, you aren't trying very hard.

- **Be as flexible as possible.** You have to cover the responsibilities, but there are a lot of reasonable requests you can grant that don't impact your ability to deliver. Pay attention to results, not to how, where, or when the work gets done.

- **Structure responsibilities around the employees.** Try to assign people work they are interested in.

- **Be alert for hints that people are unhappy.** Discuss it with them. There may be an answer that is a win all the way around.

Most managers have very little say in monetary compensation, but there are a lot of intangible things that are under the direct control of the immediate supervisor. Of the different types of power under the manager's control, money is far from the most important.

The Power of "Thank You"

Techies are just like everyone else. We want to feel like we're part of something bigger than ourselves. Find a way to present a vision of a successful team. Then, every time you have a success, send a thank you message to the responsible team members stressing what made it a success.

Successful teams are dedicated, professional, intelligent, resourceful, and resilient. "Thank you for your work on the xyz project. Your dedication and hard work were key elements to our success. When you suggested using method *abc*, you saved the company money and improved our customers' experience. You are a huge part of our team's success."

Define your team as successful. Message relentlessly about what that means. Find your team members' successes and recognize them.

Cc your own manager on these "thank you" messages; your boss needs to know what your team is doing, and employees need to understand that their contribution is seen and appreciated within the larger organization.

Awards

Awards provide a more formal way to express thanks to team members. Some successful programs allow employees to nominate each other for certificates of thanks, trophies, or even nominal cash awards. These can be presented in meetings, or even during a team lunch—how much does it cost to order in pizza, anyway?

Let your boss present the awards. That way your team members know that not only do you appreciate their contributions; they are getting visibility in the organization for their accomplishments.

Recognize success, and create a culture where people recognize each other's contributions.

Exercising Power

There are five different ways that power can be exercised within an organization:

- **Coercive power.** This is the type of power exercised by using threats or punishment to try to push the other person into doing what you want. Overuse of coercive power causes resentment and is generally less effective than other ways of exercising power.

- **Legitimate power.** Getting people to do things for you from a position of authority within the organization.

- **Expert power.** Using personal expertise or knowledge to persuade people to do what you are requesting.

- **Reward power.** This is when incentives are used to get people to do what you are asking. Studies show that certain types of reward, such as interesting work assignments or recognition, are really effective at changing behavior.

- **Referent power.** This is when people are willing to do things for you because they like you. Some charismatic leaders have been effective using referent power, but they are few and far between.

Legitimate power extends only so far. People understand that you are the boss, so you have a legitimate right to ask them to perform reasonable work. To really motivate people, you need to look further.

Proper use of rewards (such as interesting work assignments, recognition, or the opportunity to learn a new skill) can be great motivators for solid performers. Combine that with the expertise you have built up over your career, and you have an enviable ability to motivate your team.

Legitimate power (sometimes also known as "executive" power) is the most effective way to deal with certain types of emergency situations. Sometimes there just is not time to reach a consensus on the way forward.

But if you end up issuing orders too frequently, you will lose your team. They may go elsewhere. Or they may do something worse. They may stop using their own initiative and rely on you to issue orders on exactly what you need them to do. If you get to that point, your effectiveness as a team leader drops significantly.

Processes for Success

How do you track progress? How do you communicate each person's contribution to the rest of the team?

Ticketing systems, project tracking processes, team meetings, and staff schedules are all examples of processes that should be examined to see if they can be improved.

PROFESSIONAL PRIDE

Make sure that peoples' contributions to the team are visible. Some managers post visible lists or updates of what every team member is working on, and their progress toward completion. Depending on the nature of the workplace, this can be on a visible bulletin board, or on a SharePoint dashboard.

This has several benefits. It recognizes the contributions of each team member. It provides your boss a way to see what your team is doing. And it provides an incentive for people to execute their responsibilities quickly and well because everyone knows who was responsible for a particular activity.

Decision-Making Process

You also need to consider the decision-making process you are going to put in place.

Consult-and-decide means that you ask for information and input from the team, and then make a decision. This is an alternative to *building a consensus*. In general, it is worth the time to try to build a consensus if the decision is going to require enthusiastic support by your team. In situations where either the team is inexperienced or the decision needs to be made quickly, consult-and-decide is going to be the more appropriate decision-making process.

Feedback

Establish a feedback process early in your tenure. Feedback should flow both ways, from you to the team, and from the team to you.

When you provide feedback to your team, at least 75% of your feedback should be positive. If you aren't able to come up with that many nice things to say, you may need to engage in some self-examination. Very few people are that bad; most people want to learn, improve, and do a good job.

■ **Note** If you have a team member who does not pull their weight, or who consistently makes mistakes, you need to address the situation before team morale suffers. In some cases, you may decide that this person's behavior cannot be corrected, and you may need to replace this team member immediately.

Chapter 7 has some hints for issuing effective reprimands, if things have risen to that level. More frequently, a minor correction can be couched in the middle of positive feedback on the bulk of the work that the team member is doing right.

Make sure that your expectations are clear. Usually, when things aren't done the way you want, it is because your team members don't understand your expectations. If you haven't made your expectations clear or communicated them effectively, that is on you. Don't take it out on your team members.

Provide opportunities for your teammates to give you feedback. Usually, my only requests are that team members address me respectfully and in private when they need to provide me with negative feedback. If there are resentments within the team, it is better to get them out into the open and discuss them honestly. If the resentments fester in the dark, they are guaranteed to emerge in a time and place when you are least able to deal with them.

When a team member brings an issue like this to your attention, take a deep breath. If you can't deal calmly with the issue right now, thank the team member for bringing the issue to your attention, tell him or her that you want more time to think about it, and schedule a meeting for later.

Think about how you want your team member to react when he or she has negative feedback coming from you. That is how you need to react. Your people are knowledgeable professionals, and they deserve the same sort of treatment that you demand for yourself.

Organizational Culture

Stephen Robbins[3] defined several axes that can be used to define an organization's culture:

- **Member identity.** How closely people associate with the organization, rather than with subgroups within the organization.

- **Group emphasis.** Is work assigned to groups or individuals?

- **People focus.** How much weight is given to the impact of decisions on people?

- **Unit integration.** How much are units encouraged to cooperate?

- **Control.** How much do rules and policies govern behavior?

- **Risk tolerance.** Are employees encouraged to take risks to innovate?

---

[3]Stephen P. Robbins, *Organizational Behavior*, 10th ed. Upper Saddle River, NJ: Prentice Hall, 2002.

- **Reward criteria.** What sort of behavior is rewarded? Are rewards based on behavior or criteria such as seniority or popularity?

- **Conflict tolerance.** Are employees encouraged to air conflict and disagreement openly?

- **Means-end orientation.** Does management focus on means or outcomes? Organizations with a balanced approach tend to be more successful in executing complex projects.

- **Open systems focus.** Does the organization monitor and adjust to changes in the external environment?

Think about where your organization falls on these axes, and look into what type of environment your new team members come from.

You will live in the atmosphere of the larger organizational culture, but you can define an organizational culture for your team. Think about what type of team you want to lead, then think about how to get there.

Messaging from the manager can help set a tone. Think about an aspect of team culture that you want to create or emphasize, then talk about it when you discuss the team environment with each of the team members. Persuade them how the world should be, and show your team members that it is within their power to create it.

Techies tend to have very sensitive BS detectors. Don't say things that you don't mean. It is okay to explicitly tell your team members that you are messaging about something, but follow it up by explaining why you see that characteristic as important. Use your powers of persuasion, backed by a sincere commitment on your part to foster that characteristic. Your team members will respect you for it, and they will follow your lead.

Staff Training

Find room in the budget for staff training. But beyond paid coursework, encourage team members to stretch to learn from each other. Cross-training increases the value of each team member.

Training needs to take into account the strengths, weaknesses, and career goals of each person on the team. For technical people, learning new skills is a valuable reward.

To the extent possible, try to structure training on a just-in-time basis. If you have someone train on something six months before they get to touch it, they are guaranteed to have forgotten everything they learned. When someone is trained (either in the classroom, or by cross-training with a teammate), provide them an immediate opportunity to exercise their new knowledge.

In one place I worked, there was a budget that allowed for one offsite training course per person per year. The team members coordinated who would go to each class. When that person returned, they were expected to spend their first few days back documenting what they had learned and transferring the knowledge to their teammates who had been covering the environment. This saved the organization money, improved teamwork, and allowed the team members to learn far more than they would have been able to cover by hoarding knowledge.

Cross-Training

Make sure you do not have any skills or knowledge that are limited to just one person. Where you find this, consider it to be a gap. Schedule time for the specialist to bring teammates up to speed and write documentation.

Technologists like to learn new skills. This should be a road that is travelled in both directions. Everyone on the team should be both a teacher and a student in cross-training sessions. It makes it easier to provide vacation support, and it protects the organization in case someone is sick or leaves.

Credibility

The most powerful tool you will have as a manager is your own credibility. It will take time to win your team's trust. It can take you only a moment's lapse to lose it entirely.

When times get tough, credibility is going to be what gets you through. You will be able to acknowledge the problem to your team and ask for their freely given assistance in resolving it. Your credibility will be what makes the difference between getting the support you need and getting a cold shoulder.

The key to earning credibility is to keep your commitments. Try to make your commitments in writing so that you don't run into a problem with each side remembering something slightly different.

Sometimes you will make a commitment that you are prevented from keeping by circumstances beyond your control. When you discover that you will not be able to meet a commitment, come clean and renegotiate the commitment as appropriate. If things are just not going to work out, apologize. People will be upset, but they will respect you for dealing straight with them.

Commitments should not be made lightly. Other commitments will need to be taken into account. If you are making assumptions, try to state them explicitly. (I'll deliver the server next week, assuming that the hardware is delivered to me as scheduled.) If there are things that can be done to mitigate possible problems with the assumptions, it doesn't hurt to make those actions explicit as well.

You are the heart of your team. If your team can't trust you to deliver reliably, your team will not be able to deliver for you.

Your Education

Do not neglect your own education and training. I started my MS program knowing that I could only take one or two classes a year because of my work load. When I started the program, it seemed like it would take forever to finish up the program, but five years later, I had my degree.

Take the long view toward your development. Think about where you want to be in five years. If you were interviewing someone for that job today, what would you look for? What would you ask? That is the information and experience you need to pursue.

It is up to you to set the tone for your team. Make your team into a learning organization. It will make your team more flexible, and it will make your team members happier.

Read books. Find some substantive blogs to follow. Take classes. Attend lectures. And think about going after that degree you meant to finish, even if you can only take one or two classes at a time. You will be better for it. It will make you a better manager—and a better rounded person—over time.

Summary

As the leader of the team, it is your responsibility to set the tone, and to collect people around you to reinforce it. Decide what your team's personality is going to be, and recruit to shape the team into that personality.

Your actions have an outsized impact on the team dynamics. Keep in mind that the primary reason most people leave a job is because they don't like their immediate supervisor. This doesn't mean you have to be everyone's buddy; that would be counterproductive. Be professional. Be fair. Have clear expectations. Recognize excellence. And then think about how to structure your team to support the personality you want it to have.

Discussion Questions

1. Describe the characteristics you want your team to embody. Does your team have those characteristics now? How would you go about fostering those characteristics?

2. List some interview questions that would be good for finding out a candidate's technical expertise. Now list some questions that would be good for assessing the candidate's character.

3. Visible tracking of each person's progress on assigned work is both a good reward and a good motivator. What method would work well in your environment? A weekly report? A bulletin or white board? A web-based dashboard?

4. Every manager should have a personal education plan. There are technical certifications or diplomas that you can work toward. What are your educational goals? What concrete actions are you taking to achieve them?

Further Reading

Blanchard, Ken, and Spencer Johnson. *The One Minute Manager*. New York, NY: Morrow, 2003.

Harvard Business Essentials. *Manager's Toolkit*. Boston, MA: Harvard Business School Press, 2004.

Robbins, Stephen P. *Organizational Behavior*, 10th ed. Upper Saddle River, NJ: Prentice Hall, 2002.

Watkins, Michael. *The First 90 Days*. Boston, MA: Harvard Business School Press, 2003.

Resolving Conflicts

One of the less pleasant aspects of being in charge of the team is that you will need to step in to make sure that conflicts do not get in the way of the team's progress. This chapter includes some information and techniques that will be useful in dealing with conflicts.

Conflicts are not necessarily negative. People see different pieces of the entire system, and there are likely to be legitimate conflicts of interest between them. When handled properly, conflicts can lead to positive change.

DESTRUCTIVE VS. CONSTRUCTIVE CONFLICT

Destructive conflict is characterized by tension and argument. An atmosphere of antagonism and anger is likely to emerge during destructive conflict.

Constructive conflict is characterized by mutual respect and consideration. The people engaged in the conflict hear each other out and consider the alternative point of view. Constructive conflicts may not always end in agreement, but at least alternative points of view were seriously considered.

Methods of Conflict Management

There are several different ways to handle a conflict. Blake and Mouton[1] characterized them as

- **Confrontation.** In this problem-solving mode, the affected people directly confront the conflict and try to work it through. (*Confrontation* refers to confronting the problem, and it is not meant to indicate that the manager picks a fight with a team member.)

- **Compromise.** This is a give-and-take approach that tries to give each of the parties some of what they are looking for.

- **Smoothing.** This approach emphasizes areas of agreement and de-emphasizes areas of disagreement.

- **Forcing.** A "solution" is imposed from higher up the hierarchy. If this method is overused, a manager will be seen as autocratic, which may have an impact on team members being willing to exercise independent judgment.

- **Withdrawal.** The problem is ignored. This is the least desirable tactic because the problem will just fester and re-appear again.

These five methods of dealing with a problem are listed in order of effectiveness. Effective managers use confrontation and compromise most frequently. Weaker managers tend to use the other three methods of dealing with a conflict.

Conflicts between Team Members

You can't live your team members' lives for them, and you can't force them to engage in constructive rather than destructive conflict. But you can create an environment of trust, respect, and compassion.

There are a few techniques you can use to deal with an interpersonal conflict:

- Interview the people involved to try to identify the core issues.

- Separate these issues into needs and wants.

---

[1] Robert R. Blake and Jane Mouton, *The Managerial Grid: The Key to Leadership Excellence.* Houston, TX: Gulf Publishing, 1964.

- It will not be effective for you to simply pick winners and losers. (You may have to make a decision to move forward, but listen to both sides first.)

- Provide individual coaching for the people involved. Ask them to restate the other person's point of view.

- Encourage both team members to have an open mindset and try to build a fresh relationship based on tolerance and respect. They don't have to agree, just work together.

Conflicts between Teams

Conflicts sometimes emerge between teams. Sometimes these are proxy battles between the team leaders. If you are engaged in one of these, it is your responsibility to sort it out.

More frequently, there are issues associated with work allocation and scheduling. It is up to management to assign responsibilities. Negotiate with the other team lead, and engage the next level of management if there is a genuine disagreement about task ownership.

Scheduling can be more difficult. Teams need to consider how things look from the other team's point of view.

- Provide as much advance notice as possible.

- Work on the procedure collaboratively.

- Specify formats in which standard requests should be submitted. That will help avoid the problem where someone mentions something to someone else at lunch, which is inevitably either misunderstood or forgotten.

Sometimes there are members of each team who are friendly. To the extent possible, leverage these personal relationships to foster trust and cooperation between the groups.

The fact is that the teams have to work together. It is in everyone's best interest to develop compatible work habits.

Personality Types

The most common way to characterize personality types is the Myers–Briggs Type Indicator.[2] There are four axes used to measure a person's personality:

- **Extrovert/Introvert (E/I)**: Do you draw energy by interacting with other people (E)? Or by thinking and studying during your private time (I)?

- **Sensation/Intuition (S/N)**: Do you gather information by direct observation (S)? Or are you more intuitive and conceptual (N)?

- **Thinking/Feeling (T/F)**: Do you reach decisions by thinking and logic (T)? Or do you use more subjective and personal criteria to reach decisions (F)?

- **Judgment/Perception (J/P)**: Do you value completion, deadlines, and closure (J)? Or do you see things as more of an ongoing process, with deadlines being flexible and fungible goals (P)?

When psychologists run population studies of personality types, some interesting patterns occur. It turns out that there are differences between techies and the general population, and even between different types of techies.[3]

There was no significant difference between IS people and the general population on the J/P axis. About half of each group falls onto each end of the axis. But there are significant differences on the other three axes.

Among IS developers 75% were introverts, 80% were on the thinking end of the spectrum, and 55% were classified as intuitive. That contrasts with 25%, 50%, and 25%, respectively, for the general population. (That helps explain part of the communication gap between implementation teams and the end-user community.)

If you think about the people you are dealing with, you might see where some communication disconnects can occur. If you are an "N," but you are working with someone who is an "S," you need to present information to that person differently than you would want it presented to yourself. Perhaps something more concrete, such as a prototype or mock-up, would work better than a conceptual overview.

There are other ways to look at how people interact. Psychologist David Merrill (a codeveloper of the Wilson Learning Social Styles Profile) characterizes social styles as being defined along axes of assertiveness (proactive/

---

[2]Isabel Briggs Myers with Peter B. Myers, *Gifts Differing: Understanding Personality Type.* Mountain View, CA: Davies-Black Publishing, 1980/1995.
[3]Kathy Schwalbe, *Information Technology Project Management.* Boston, MA: Thompson, 2006.

reactive) and responsiveness (task oriented/people oriented).[4] The four social styles in this classification are

- **Drivers** are proactive and task oriented. They tend to be rooted in the present, and look at actions over words. They can be viewed as pushy or dominating.

- **Expressives** are proactive and people oriented. They look to the future, and try to find new perspectives and approaches to problems. They can be viewed as manipulating or ambitious.

- **Analyticals** are reactive and task oriented. They are thinkers, and tend to look to the past for lessons. They can be viewed as critical and indecisive.

- **Amiables** are reactive and people oriented. They are strongly relationship driven. They can be viewed as conforming and ingratiating.

Thinking about the social styles of the people you are dealing with can help you to approach them more successfully. The strongest team will be made up of people of different styles because a team of similar people is likely to overlook something important.

Dealing with Difficult People

There are a few keys to dealing with a difficult person:

- Identify what you feel. Your feelings will cause you to think and perceive things a certain way, which may or may not be entirely accurate. If you identify what you feel, you can correct for your emotional filter and make sure your perceptions are correct.

- In what ways are you contributing to the conflict? It takes two to tango. Think about the ways in which the conflict is partly your fault. Do you sometimes behave in a manipulative way to force the issue? Or gossip about the other person?

- What assumptions are you making about the other person? These may be coloring your perceptions, and may be contributing to the conflict.

- To what extent are you causing the problem?

---

[4]David W. Merrill and Roger H. Reid, *Personal Styles and Effective Performance*. Boca Raton, FL: CRC Press, 1981.

This doesn't mean that you have to be a patsy. Don't let anyone take your power away from you. That will just cause resentment and keep the conflict going anyway. Just don't feed into it, and do your best to make the situation work.

If you can remove the emotion from the conflict, you can get closer to addressing the actual problem. Try considering some questions to define the problem:

- What is the problem? State it in the simplest, least emotional way possible.

- Whose feelings are upset? What are they feeling? Why?

- Who raised the issue? Why?

Once you have defined the problem, you are that much closer to being able to work with the other person to resolve it. Examine the issue unemotionally, and try to view the issue from the other person's point of view to find some possible workarounds.

Don't Be a Difficult Person

We have been discussing how you should shape your communication to fit the other person's personality and social style better. Do you get prickly if people are communicating with you in other than your preferred style?

To some extent, you need to get over it. You are a leader, and part of being a leader is sucking it up and not sweating the small stuff.

Now that we've got that out of the way, maybe we can find ways to structure communication in a way that is more comfortable for you. If you clearly communicate how different requests should come to you (what information you need, what format you need it in, and how you would like it delivered), you can control some of the communication, and you can get the information you need in a format that is comfortable for you.

Communications Breakdowns

When there is no communication, progress ceases. In fact, the problems will get worse if the communications breakdown is not addressed.

Communication problems can be addressed by following some good habits:

- **Clarify assumptions.** Make sure that you are both talking about the same thing.

- **Set ground rules.** You are not going to be able to solve every problem immediately. Pick a problem and work on it.

- **Share information.** If you have information that is relevant to the subject at hand, make sure that everyone involved in the conflict understands what is at stake.

- **Listen.** Hear what the other person is saying. Ask clarifying questions as needed. Make sure you understand the key points being made by the other person.

- **Avoid personal attacks.** Stick to the business problem at hand.

You may not become best friends with the other person, but you have to find a way to work together. Don't allow communications to break down. Use every tool at your disposal to find a way to work together.

Issuing Reprimands

Nobody wants to be a jerk. Issuing reprimands stinks. But sometimes it has to be done.

The key is that it should be done quickly, clearly, privately, and personally. Don't repeat yourself ad nauseam, and prepare what you need to say beforehand. The key elements of an effective reprimand are[5]

- Make sure you have the correct information beforehand. This includes the instructions you had previously issued on the subject.

- The team member should know beforehand that you will be discussing this particular incident.

- Reprimand the team member immediately, at the beginning of the session. Be specific about what the team member did wrong, and how it should have been handled. Be brief, but be specific.

- Tell the team member how you feel about the situation. Again, be brief, but be specific.

- Pause so that it sinks in.

- Make it clear that the reprimand is over. Shake hands or make contact in an appropriate way. Tell the team member how much you value them, just not their behavior in this particular case.

---

[5]Ken Blanchard and Spencer Johnson, *The One Minute Manager*. New York, NY: Morrow, 2003.

After the reprimand is done, you need to let the matter go. No snarky comments later, no discussion with other team members, nothing.

Keep in mind that most of what your team member provides for the team is excellent work. (If that is not true, I'm not sure why you haven't removed this person from the team already.) You may need to remind the team member about the general quality of his or her work at the end of the session.

The One Minute Manager (see "Further Reading") has an excellent chapter on issuing reprimands. I highly recommend picking the book up and reading it for ideas on how to motivate your team members.

Summary

Resolving conflicts is not a type of leadership that comes easily to most technical people. A lot of technical managers avoid conflicts rather than confronting them and pushing through to a resolution.

Don't fall into the trap of allowing conflicts to manage you. Manage the environment. Deal with the conflicts directly and with integrity.

Discussion Questions

1. Think about a workplace conflict that you were engaged in. What do you think the personality type of the other person was? (Remember that "J" does not stand for "Jerk.") What is yours? How did that contribute to the conflict?

2. What are some positive ways to deal with a constructive conflict?

Further Reading

Blake, Robert R., and Jane Mouton. *The Managerial Grid: The Key to Leadership Excellence*. Houston, TX: Gulf Publishing, 1964.

Blanchard, Ken, and Spencer Johnson. *The One Minute Manager*. New York, NY: Morrow, 2003.

Harvard Business Essentials. *Manager's Toolkit*. Boston, MA: Harvard Business School Press, 2004.

Schwalbe, Kathy. *Information Technology Project Management* (Chapter 9). Boston, MA: Thompson, 2006.

Budgets

Nobody likes writing up budgets. It is a lot less fun than learning a new technology or architecting a new service. But the organization you work for needs to bring in more money than it sends out, or it is in trouble.

In IT, we are usually on the cost side of the ledger. That means that we have to be sensitive to the business cycles of the organization, and we may need to adjust our spending over the course of the year to match the business's cash flow. Work closely with the finance department to find out what the business needs, and try to structure spending to match what the company needs. If you develop a good working relationship with the finance department, it will pay off both for the business and also for your flexibility in managing your department.

Purpose of a Budget

Budgets allow the organization to plan for large expenditures. They can be used to identify where money is being spent, which is useful when planning priorities.

No matter what type of organization you work for, I can guarantee that it wants to spend less money. By identifying where money is being spent, we can start selecting targets for closer examination. The easiest place to start is on the larger budget items.

A lot of times, those costs are viewed as "fixed," but maybe the situation needs to be looked at closer. If you're spending a lot of money on hardware support, for example, maybe you should look at whether you can propose an upgrade or consolidation that could result in a net reduction in those costs. (When you're dealing with older gear, the cost of support can actually be larger than the cost of payments on new or leased equipment on an annualized basis.)

It can help to try to be creative. Perhaps you can look at moving something to the cloud or virtualizing on a smaller number of servers.

The whole process starts with identifying where you are spending your money. When Willie Sutton, the famous bank robber, was asked why he robbed banks, he said "because that's where the money is." When we find out where the money is flowing out of the organization, we know which areas to target first.

Estimating Costs

Usually, we can use the current year's expenditures as a baseline for our initial budget. There are some obvious problems with this because some costs change year to year. But you have to start somewhere, and at least the current year's expenditures will give us a list of costs that need to be examined.

Costs should be estimated for as far forward as possible, not just for the current budget cycle. If there will be a significant increase in costs next year (due to warranty expiration or an End of Service Life (EOSL) component, for example), the plans for dealing with that issue should be put in place now.

When projects or changes are proposed, the savings, profits, and costs should all be estimated for the lifetime of the project.

Different types of estimates are expected to have different margins of error:

- **Rough order of magnitude (ROM) estimate.** This is sometimes referred to as a "ballpark estimate" or a "wild-ass guess" (WAG). These are frequently provided to give management an idea whether to proceed with scoping out a project, before the details of the project have been determined. The expected accuracy of a ROM estimate is usually from 25% below to 75% above the provided estimate.

- **Budgetary estimate.** This type of estimate is made after the project's preliminary scope is known, but before the full scope and detailed budget analysis is complete. The purpose of this type of estimate is to provide numbers for long-term budget planning. A budgetary estimate is expected to be within 25% of the final number.

- **Definitive estimate.** This type of estimate is expected to be accurate to within 10%, and is made after a full budgetary analysis.

Three different ways to perform a budgetary analysis are to

- **Estimate by analogy.** Use other similar projects as a baseline for cost estimates. These estimates rely on the project manager to understand the approximate costs of differences between the projects.

- **Bottom-up estimate.** Find the cost for all the components and add the costs together. Assuming that everything is accounted for, this should yield the most accurate result.

- **Parametric estimate.** These estimates are based on another estimated parameter, frequently lines of code or function points. These estimates can be surprisingly accurate, assuming that the estimate for the lines of code was correct, and that the baseline information is accurate.

It is common for project managers to use a combination of these techniques as a confidence-building measure that the estimates are in the right neighborhood.

The obvious danger of a cost estimate is that human beings are prone to underestimate because we are wired to want to please management. On the one hand, we have to protect against this by being as complete as possible and allowing an adequate cushion for contingencies. On the other hand, inflating cost estimates too far can lead to a job being over bid and lost, or can result in a project being cancelled when the ROI (return on investment) analysis is unfavorable.

Quality Management

Defects are disproportionately expensive. If defects can be eliminated, it helps reduce overall costs. Quality management can be an important part of cost management.

Quality management also applies to cost estimates that are provided to business. The way to improve the quality of those estimates is to track the variance between estimates and reality over time, and use postmortems to identify where the variances come from.

As with most other things you manage, you will get results in areas that you measure. Measure quality, track it, set your team's goals in terms of quality, and you will be able to improve it.

Negotiating Your Team's Budget

There are several things you should do to improve your success in negotiating an adequate budget for your team:

- Find out about the organization's budget cycles and process. Identify the guidelines and deadlines you are expected to follow. Your peers and your boss are good people to find this information from.

- Find out if there are cash flow issues and spending timing issues that you need to be sensitive to.

- Get to know the finance people who are responsible for your team's budget. Find out from them what their concerns are, and see if there is a better way to communicate your requirements, or to address their requirements.

- What are the real concerns underlying the budget cycle?

- Who are the decision makers? Make sure they understand what you are doing to control costs and improve efficiency.

- Understand every line item of your team's budget. If you don't, follow up with your team members who manage that facility. Every expense should be associated with a particular facility that you are responsible for.

- Start gathering the information well in advance of the deadlines. Ask for quotes from your vendors, and assign team members to compare the renewal quotes to the current inventory of facilities you are responsible for. If they discover big savings, keep track of them, and give that staff member credit in a thank you email with your boss cc'd. Keep track of that information for their annual review. If you show your staff that you value cost savings, they will respond.

- As actual numbers and estimates start coming in, compare them to what you expected. Understand the differences.

- Push back on vendors who seem out of line; some vendors view a new manager as an easy mark. Get alternate quotes, and let the vendors know that there is a new sheriff in town.

Organizing the Information You Need

Everything starts with inventories of systems and software. Once you have those in place, estimate the costs associated with each system and each software license.

Then look for low-hanging fruit where reorganization or retirement can have a significant cost savings.

Make sure that your team members understand that they are responsible for keeping their part of the inventory up to date. Also ask them to look for cost savings opportunities by decommissioning old facilities, and make sure that they get credit when they find them. When your staff members look good, it makes you look good. Make it worth their while to make you look good by giving them credit for what they do right.

Tracking Costs and Benefits

The methods your finance team uses to track costs and benefits will be different from organization to organization. Work with your finance team to provide them the information in the format that is most useful for them.

Total Cost of Ownership (TCO)

The total cost of a system needs to be estimated for the entire lifetime of the system. If this number is not reported accurately and included in planning, management will not have planned properly for large increases in maintenance or licensing costs that may appear in the out-years.

By looking at the total cost, you also avoid problems with sales reps shifting costs into the out-years of a contract. That may help you look like a hero in the short term, but it will be very costly to the company over the long haul.

When I compare the costs for two solutions, I try to nail down all the hardware, software, support, environmental, training, and intangible costs. The total package for each of the proposed solutions should be compared over the lifetime of the project. (In my experience, five years is a good time window, if the lifetime of the system hasn't been specified elsewhere.) I frequently find that the solution with the smallest upfront costs is among the more expensive once you consider the support and environmental costs in the fourth and fifth year of the contract.

Cash Flow Analysis

A cash flow analysis looks at the current benefits the organization gets from a system versus the costs of keeping it running. This sort of analysis does not take into account the sunk costs (what has already been spent) involved in bringing the system online.

Tangible costs and benefits are those that are easily counted in monetary terms. Accounting for intangible costs and benefits is obviously much harder. Intangible benefits may be something like prestige, publicity, or ease of use. Some of these can be estimated as dollar amounts, but the analysis will necessarily be more subjective than with tangible costs and benefits.

Depending on the reason why you are running the analysis, intangible costs and benefits may or may not need to be reported or estimated. When you are asked to perform an analysis, try to pin down how intangible costs and benefits should be accounted for.

Direct and Indirect Costs and Benefits

There will also be direct and indirect costs and benefits to account for. An example of an indirect cost would be the electric bill to run air conditioning to the server room. These costs could be significant, and some effort should be made to include them in cost analyses. (One way of estimating the cost is to find out what the annual electric bill is for the data center, and estimate what percentage of the equipment in the data center is associated with a particular system. You can use a somewhat naïve estimate, for example, dividing by the total number of racks in the data center or something similar, but at least you will have a magnitude estimate.)

Procurement

Sales representatives will usually follow your lead. Make sure they know what will get your business, and make sure that your criteria make sense for the business. Some things I look for from sales reps are

- Accurate, timely information.
- Solid project knowledge (usually from the sales rep's engineering staff).
- Tries to understand the challenges my organization faces.
- Presents alternatives when appropriate.
- Offers engineering assistance as needed to help size or scope the environment properly.

- Interested in a long-term rather than a short-term relationship.

- Recognizes that a reliable customer who provides references is worth a significant discount.

Some suppliers do not want to provide a quote for five years of support, or cannot provide solid quotes for the costs of expected upgrades three years in the future. In those cases, I try to insist on rider to the purchase contract with "not-to-exceed" pricing in the out-years. I'm not the only one who does this, and most vendors understand what I am after once I raise the issue. Sometimes the sales rep has to escalate the issue to a regional manager to get approval for these riders, but they are not usually a problem once they understand that you are serious about them.

Supplier Stability

Examine the stability of your suppliers when you make purchases. Check out their financials as if you were buying their stock. In practice, your company is making an investment in the supplier company. If the supplier goes out of business, who is going to provide patches, service, and upgrades? Get a handle on whether the company is stable, and whether they are a likely acquisition target by someone who will abandon the product line you are purchasing.

Ethics

When you make recommendations for a large purchase, there is a lot of money on the table. Sometimes you will be felt out to see if you would be more sympathetic if some of that money fell into your pocket. Don't do it. It is illegal. More important, it is wrong.

I know people who have been offered a golf vacation in Bermuda or a new sports car to help a vendor land a seven-figure contract. In these cases, the offers were reported to their management, were discussed between the legal teams for the two companies, and negotiations suddenly involved some extra safeguards and concessions by the vendor.

Your organization has a policy for dealing with gifts from vendors, and a procedure for reporting bribe attempts. If you are put in this position, follow that procedure to the letter. Do not allow your good name and career to be destroyed for a few baubles.

Summary

Budgeting is not something that most technology people like to do. It is one of the tasks that tends to be procrastinated until the last minute. This results in sloppy results, which lead to lots of midyear groveling to get "extra" money for that service contract renewal you forgot about.

The place to start is with an accurate inventory, including systems, software, ongoing projects, and expected projects. Once you have a good understanding for where your money is going, you can both provide accurate estimates for the coming year as well as finding opportunities for saving your organization's money.

Discussion Questions

1. What is the budget cycle for your organization? When do you need to hand in your preliminary budget? When is the final budget approved?

2. What method does your organization use to estimate costs and benefits?

3. Does your organization use charge-backs? How are they tracked? Is your inventory being charged back to the right departments?

4. One tactic for improving budget quality is to "finish" the budget two weeks before it is due, then review it again shortly before submission. What advantages do you see to this tactic?

Further Reading

Harvard Business Essentials. *Manager's Toolkit*. Boston, MA: Harvard Business School Press, 2004.

Schwalbe, Kathy. *Information Technology Project Management* (Chapters 7, 12). Boston, MA: Thompson, 2006.

Root Cause Analysis

Troubleshooting Problems

Troubleshooting refers to the methods used to resolve problems. People who troubleshoot a lot come up with a set of habits, methods, and tools to help with the process. These provide a standard approach for gathering the necessary information to zero in on the cause of a problem. This standard approach is known as a *methodology*.

Methodologies save time while troubleshooting. They allow us to organize our efforts to devote every available resource to resolving the problem.

But a methodology only saves time when applied intelligently. It is possible to become so devoted to the process that we forget the purpose of the whole exercise—fixing the problem. It makes no sense to spend all our time writing logs and no time testing hypotheses.

Good methodologies contain tools for coordinating efforts and organizing the troubleshooting process. The key is to focus our time and resources, minimize the cost of the problem, and find and fix the root cause. The effectiveness of these tools has been studied and verified (see, for example, Doggett in "Further Reading").

Unfortunately, many otherwise good technical people try to minimize the time spent resolving a problem by ignoring the process structure and documentation. Structure keeps us from going in circles. Documentation provides useful information for avoiding wasted effort, fixing future problems, or evolving the design of our data environment.

Proper documentation also allows less experienced staff members to duplicate our methods and procedures. This is a key concern where these junior staff members are the primary support staff for vacation coverage or disaster recovery operations. (Who wants to get called off a beach in Florida to resolve a problem in the home office? Some short-sighted administrators regard this scenario as job security. More mature admins regard it as a nuisance.)

Our techniques need to be seen as tools to be used to solve a problem. Not every home repair involves a wrecking bar and sledgehammer, and not every problem requires a full Ishikawa diagram and formal set of probability calculations. With experience and maturity comes the judgment to decide which tools are appropriate for a particular problem. We have to practice the techniques so that we know how and where they will be most useful. Short-cutting the process unduly just causes problems in the long run.

In broad outline, troubleshooting consists of three phases: Investigation, Analysis, and Implementation. Presentations of troubleshooting methodologies sometimes present these steps with slightly different names, or emphasize slightly different aspects of the process, but the steps in Table 9-1 are one way to organize the process.

Table 9-1. The Troubleshooting Process

Step	Comments
Investigation phase	
Problem statement	A clear, concise statement of the problem
Problem description	List the symptoms of the problem, including what works and what doesn't; identify the scope and importance of the problem
Identify differences and changes	What has changed recently? How does this system differ from working systems?
Analysis phase	
Brainstorm	Gather hypotheses: what might have caused the problem?
Rank the likely causes	How likely is each hypothesis?
Test the hypotheses	Schedule testing for the most likely hypothesis; perform nondisruptive testing immediately
Implementation phase	
Apply the fix	Complete the repair
Verify the fix	Make sure the problem is really resolved
Document the resolution	Save the troubleshooting information; get a sign-off from the service owner

In this chapter, the examples will be centered around troubleshooting computer system errors, which is something that technical teams need to do fairly often. The same techniques can be used to troubleshoot any type of problem, including organizational problems.

Investigation Phase

The Investigation phase consists of steps to identify the nature of the problem, gather information describing it, and find distinctions between working and nonworking states of the system. The defining characteristic of the Investigation phase is the collection of facts, not opinions.

For nontrivial problems, we save time over the long run by not jumping immediately to Analysis or Implementation. There is usually a lot of pressure to "just do something." Unfortunately, that is not the most effective use of time or resources. There is a universe of harmful or irrelevant actions that we can take, and only a very few actions that will improve or fix the situation.

Problem Statement

At the beginning of the process, we need to name the problem. A good problem statement defines the problem in a broad enough way that it accurately portrays the effects of the problem, but is narrow enough to focus our problem analysis.

Value judgments have no place in a problem statement. The goal of a problem statement is to produce a concise, correct, high-level description of the problem. To do this, focus on what did happen versus what should have happened.

Ideally, the problem statement will specify a defect in a particular object or service. The problem statement should answer the questions, "Where is the problem?" and "What is wrong?"

Problem Description

Once we have named the problem, we need to list as many symptoms as possible without becoming redundant. In particular, we should list dissimilar symptoms—their juxtaposition allows us to look at common threads between them.

It may even be helpful to list the things that are working fine, as contrasted with items that do not work.

The start and end times of an outage should be nailed down as accurately as possible. This allows us to ask "What changed?" on a precise time window. We need this information for the next stage of the troubleshooting process.

We also need to get a handle on the scope and importance of the problem. Although these might not be directly related to the root cause of the problem, they will determine the types of tests and resolutions that we might consider to resolve the problem.

The importance of the problem will also determine how many resources we can spend in troubleshooting it. IT abounds with problems too expensive or too trivial to resolve. The role of IT is usually to notify the decision makers with appropriate estimates of costs and consequences of a problem or its resolution. Business requirements and resources will determine which of the universe of problems will get our full attention.

Identify Differences and Changes

If we can compare the broken system to one that is not broken, we can see what is different. If we can identify what changed just before it became broken, that is important information too.

Analysis Phase

The Analysis phase is focused on taking the facts from the Investigation phase and explaining them. In this phase, we generate hypotheses from the information we have gathered, test the hypotheses, and report the results.

This stage of the troubleshooting process is all about the scientific method. Intuition and experience focus the investigation by identifying which possibilities are most likely to provide a solution.

Brainstorm: Gather Hypotheses

The Brainstorming step is where we try to identify all possible causes of the problem. We use the facts from the Investigation phase to generate hypotheses about the cause of the problem.

The symptoms and problem statement can be turned around to provide hypotheses. We ask ourselves questions such as "How can this item have caused this problem?" The answers can be added to our list of hypotheses.

It is sometimes useful to have a system diagram or other mental model of the system before thinking about possible causes. Each component of the system should be considered as a possible cause.

(A common example of such a mental model is the Open Systems Interconnection (OSI) network stack in Table 9-2. Some network troubleshooting methodologies focus on eliminating portions of the stack as the cause of the problem.)

Table 9-2. OSI Network Reference Model—Example of a System Model

Level Name	Description
Application layer	Application programs using the network
Presentation layer	Data presentation to the applications
Session layer	Manages sessions between cooperating applications
Transport layer	End-to-end error detection and correction
Network layer	Manages connections and addressing on the network
Data Link layer	Reliable data delivery across physical network components
Physical layer	Network physical media

In this context, "components" need to be considered at an appropriate level of abstraction. Depending on the nature of the problem, a diode, a computer, a network service, or the Internet may be considered to be components. For our purposes, we define a *component* as an entity that we can test and then eliminate as the source of the problem.

If we can eliminate a component, it makes no sense to spend time eliminating subcomponents. The level of abstraction can make a huge difference in the amount of time spent in a troubleshooting exercise. (In an idealized situation where we can eliminate half of the system at each step, for example, we can narrow a problem down to one component out of a million in only 20 steps.) Figure 9-1 illustrates several different levels of abstraction that might be used to examine a problem.

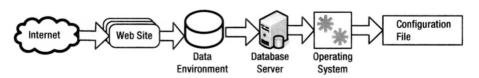

Figure 9-1. Levels of abstraction

There are several tools to help organize brainstorming sessions. One such tool is the Ishikawa cause-and-effect diagram (see the "Ishikawa Cause-and-Effect Diagrams" sidebar). A key to a successful brainstorming session (especially one involving a team of people) is that everyone focuses on identifying possible causes rather than starting to drill down on a particular hypothesis. Ishikawa diagrams help to make sure that each system component is examined as a possible cause of the problem.

ISHIKAWA CAUSE-AND-EFFECT DIAGRAMS

Ishikawa cause-and-effect (or "Fishbone") diagrams are tools that allow us to focus a brainstorming session. We generate an Ishikawa diagram by drawing a "backbone" arrow pointing to the right at a rectangle containing our problem statement. Then attach four to six "ribs," each of which represents a major broad category of items that may contribute to the problem. Each of our components should fit on one or another of these ribs.

The next step can be done by the troubleshooting team leader or by the whole team. Specific causes are attached to the appropriate rib, and more detailed potential causes are listed as branches of their related causes.

Figure 9-2 shows an example of an Ishikawa diagram. The four categories chosen for this diagram were "Computer System," "Computing Environment," "People and Procedures," and "Application." Several secondary potential causes have been attached to each of the main categories.

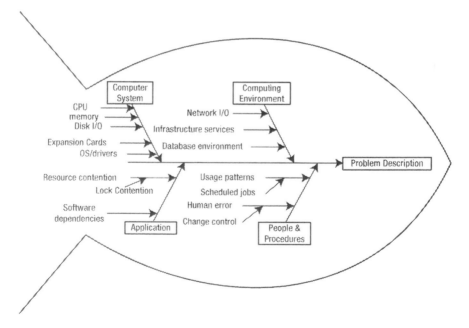

Figure 9-2. Ishikawa cause-and-effect diagram

Appropriate primary categories for the diagram may be different from situation to situation. Common paradigms presented in the literature include "materials, methods, machines, and manpower" or "people, procedures, plant, and parts." Whatever we choose, our major categories should represent the universe of issues that may have caused our problem.

The main advantage of an Ishikawa diagram for our purposes is that it can organize the brainstorming process so significant hypotheses are not ignored. A well-organized diagram can focus the troubleshooting team's attention on each potential issue to help avoid the problem of overlooked hypotheses.

Remember that your goal is not the production of a pretty diagram. The Ishikawa diagram is a tool to facilitate brainstorming. The goal is to make sure to cover all the possible causes of our stated problem.

Not every problem requires anything as formal or organized as an Ishikawa diagram. There is no point in trying to swat a fly with a sledgehammer. But when a problem is big enough to involve multiple people and several different areas of inquiry, something similar to an Ishikawa diagram provides needed structure to a brainstorming session.

Rank the Likely Causes

Once we have a list of possible explanations for the problem, we need to decide which of them are most likely to be correct. We also need to look into any assumptions that are implicit in the hypothesis statements.

Only eliminate hypotheses when they are absolutely disproved. This step is about ranking the probabilities of the different hypotheses being the correct explanation. Unlikely hypotheses should not be discarded, though they may be characterized as "very unlikely" or "corner cases."

In some cases, the best way to test the hypotheses is by looking at information gathered during the Investigation phase. For example, a bug report may closely match the symptomology of your problem. If this is the case, we should look closely at that bug report.

For more complex problems with more moving parts, it may be useful to use formal tools to help identify which potential causes are more important than others. Interrelationship diagrams (see the "Interrelationship Diagrams" sidebar) are tools developed to help organize and think about the relationships between these potential causes. They are useful in looking for ultimate versus proximate causes.

(Ultimate causes are the "root" causes of the problem. While they may not be directly indicated by the symptoms, we will continue to have these problems until we address the ultimate causes. Proximate causes are the causes of the problem that are immediately, directly responsible for the symptoms.)

As with the Ishikawa diagrams, not every problem will require the use of this sort of formal technique. On the other hand, complex problems with lots of moving parts may benefit from their use.

INTERRELATIONSHIP DIAGRAMS

Interrelationship diagrams (IDs) are tools used to look at a collection of possible explanations and identify which of them might be a root cause. IDs are particularly useful when hypotheses are interrelated in nontrivial ways. Their purpose is to identify which of several interrelated items are causes and which are effects.

IDs use boxes containing phrases describing the potential causes. Arrows between the potential causes represent influence relationships between the issues. Each relationship can only have an arrow in one direction. (Where the relationship's influence runs in both directions, the troubleshooters must decide which one is most relevant.) Items with more "out" arrows than "in" arrows are causes. Items with more "in" arrows are effects.

Figure 9-3 shows a simple example of an Interrelationship diagram. The real benefit of an ID comes when we are looking at the relationships between the possible causes. In particular, they are helpful in distinguishing between the apparent (proximate) causes and the root (ultimate) causes.

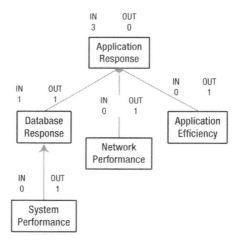

Figure 9-3. Interrelationship diagram

Researchers provide several suggestions for using IDs effectively:[1]

- Collect information from multiple distinct sources.

- Phrases with a noun and a verb are recommended in each box.

- Diagrams must reflect a group consensus.

---

[1]Sigeru Mizuno, ed.. *Management for Quality Improvement: The 7 New QC Tools.* Cambridge, England: Productivity Press, 1988.

- Redo diagrams several times if necessary.
- Don't get distracted by intermediate factors.

A common way to use IDs is to write each box's description on a Post-It note, arrange them on a white board, and draw in the arrows. This can be a useful way to deal with a large number of interrelated hypotheses.

In more complicated implementations, arrows may be weighted to try and rank the causes in order of importance. As a practical matter, that is probably overkill for most troubleshooting exercises of the sort that system administrators face.

Usually, the diagram's main benefit is in helping the troubleshooting team to focus on the issues and their relationships. In particular, it helps distinguish between the causes and symptoms of a problem. The relative importance of the competing hypotheses and the relationships between them are often a side-benefit of this discussion.

Test the Hypotheses

Once we have identified which hypotheses are most likely to be correct, we need to schedule them for testing immediately. This does not necessarily mean that they can actually be tested immediately. Some hypotheses require disruptive testing, which may need to be scheduled during a maintenance window. Nevertheless, testing should be scheduled immediately for any hypotheses that are considered likely to be the cause of the problem.

Other hypotheses do not require disruptive testing. Those tests should be carried out immediately, from most likely to least likely.

As with doctors, the rule for troubleshooters is "First, do no harm." Our testing should be the least disruptive possible under the circumstances. We need to minimize costs associated with downtime, service instability, time, money, and technical resources. We should never do anything without knowing how to reverse the change.

If a fail-over solution exists, we should fail over. At a minimum, service outages should be confined to scheduled maintenance windows where possible. Data needs to be backed up to prevent data loss. In particular, configurations should be preserved before they are changed. No test should be carried out that cannot be reversed.

In some cases, it may be possible to test the hypothesis directly in some sort of test environment. This may be as simple as running an alternative copy of a program without overwriting the original. Or it may be as complex as setting up a near copy of the faulted system in a test lab. If a realistic test can be carried out without too great a cost in terms of money or time, it can assure us that we have identified the root cause of the problem.

Depending on the situation, it may even be appropriate to test out the hypotheses by directly applying the fix. If this approach is used, it is important to only perform one test at a time, and back out the results of each failed hypotheses before trying the next one. Otherwise, you will not have a good handle on the root cause of the problem, and you may never be confident that it will not re-emerge at the worst possible moment.

As we design tests, we should try to have a "smoking gun" level of certainty about whether we have nailed the cause (or at least narrowed it down).

It is frequently best to start with the most likely cause for the failure, based on the troubleshooting team's understanding of the system. The history of similar faults may also indicate the most likely problem. The "most likely first" approach is especially valuable if one of the possible causes is considered to be much more likely than the others.

On the other hand, if investigating the most likely cause requires disruptive or expensive testing, it makes sense to eliminate some of the possibilities that are easier to test. This is particularly the case if there are several easily testable hypotheses.

The best approach is to schedule testing of the most likely hypotheses immediately. Then start to perform any nondisruptive or minimally disruptive testing of hypotheses. If several of the most likely hypotheses can be tested nondisruptively, so much the better. Start with them.

The key is to start eliminating possibilities as soon as possible. It makes no sense to waste time arguing about the most likely cause. Prove it. At this stage, the troubleshooting team has spent a lot of time thinking about the problem. Don't start with the corner cases, but start narrowing the list down.

Intermittent problems are especially difficult to troubleshoot. See the "Dealing with Intermittent Problems" sidebar for suggestions on handling this type of problem.

DEALING WITH INTERMITTENT PROBLEMS

Intermittent problems are extremely difficult to troubleshoot. Any reproducible problem can be troubleshot, if for no other reason than that each false possibility can be disproved. Problems that are not reproducible cannot be approached in the same way.

We will not know that a problem is not reproducible until after we have tested the available hypotheses. Hopefully, we will have been able to definitively eliminate some of the areas of concern with our testing regime. The first thing that we need to do is to see if we can knock out other possible causes with additional testing.

Problems present themselves as intermittent for one of two reasons:

We have not identified the real cause of the problem.

The problem is being caused by failing or flaky hardware.

The first possibility should be addressed by going back to the brainstorming step. It may be helpful to bring a fresh perspective into the brainstorming session, either by bringing in different people, or by sleeping on the problem.

The second problem is tougher. There are hardware diagnostics tests that can be run to try to identify the failing piece of hardware. The first thing to do is to perform general maintenance on the system. Re-seat memory chips, processors, expansion boards, and hard drives. Use an approved vacuum cleaner to clean the dust out of the case. Look for cracked traces or stress fractures on the system boards.

If OS patches are out of date, it also makes sense to apply a current patch set to resolve driver issues that may have since been fixed. Keep track of which patches are applied when so that we can back them out if new problems emerge.

Once general maintenance has been performed, test suites can perform stress-testing on a system to try to trigger the failure and identify the failing part. Ideally, we want to pull the failing system out of production long enough to be able to run the tests and perform the repair. Perhaps this can be done during a maintenance period or the system can be replaced temporarily with a piece of failover hardware.

It may be the case, however, that the costs associated with this level of troubleshooting are prohibitive. In this case, we may want to attempt to shotgun the problem.

Shotgunning is the practice of replacing potentially failing parts without having identified them as actually being flaky. In general, parts are replaced by price point, with the cheapest parts being replaced first. (See Litt in "Further Reading" section) Though we are likely to inadvertently replace working parts, the cost of the replacement may be cheaper than the costs of the alternatives (as in the downtime cost associated with stress testing).

When parts are removed during shotgunning, it is important to discard them rather than keep them as spares. Any part you remove as part of a troubleshooting exercise is questionable. (After all, what if a power surge caused multiple parts to fail? Or what if there was a cascading failure?) It does not make sense to have questionable parts in inventory; such parts would be useless for troubleshooting, and putting questionable parts into service just generates additional downtime down the road.

Shotgunning may violate your service contract if performed without the knowledge and consent of our service provider. (To get consent, it may be necessary to apply leverage to the service provider by speaking candidly with a manager about the impact of the problem and whether the provider's usual strategies are working. It may even be necessary to purchase the parts ourselves to perform shotgunning.)

Regardless of the methods used to deal with an intermittent problem, we must keep good records. Relationships between our problem and other events may only become clear when we look at patterns over time. We may only be confident that we have really resolved the problem if we can demonstrate that we've gone well beyond the usual re-occurrence frequency without the problem re-emerging.

Implementation Phase

The Implementation phase is where we finally resolve the problem. Here is where we recover the system to a working state. This is also the phase where we make sure that we have really fixed the problem and where we document our results.

Apply the Fix

Once our testing has identified the source of the problem, we need to fix it. This includes fixing any required documentation or similar configurations on other systems.

A key concern in applying the fix is that we do so in the least-disruptive, lowest-cost manner possible. (Lowest cost means that we have to consider all the costs. This includes the cost of downtime on the affected service, the cost of continued instability on the system prior to the fix, as well as direct costs associated with the repair.)

Ideally, we want to carry out the fix in a way that we can verify that the problem is actually resolved. Especially where reboots are required, it is sometimes hard to tell whether the problem has actually been fixed, or whether the reboot just cleared up the symptoms.

Verify the Fix

We need to make sure that we have actually resolved the problem. We also need to verify that we have not introduced any new problems.

In a well-organized environment, each service should have a test procedure or test suite associated with it to identify when the service is working properly. Test suites will never be 100% complete, but they can evolve into extremely useful tools. As new failure modes emerge, tests for them must be integrated into the suite.

Part of this step may be a root cause analysis to make sure that we have nailed the cause of the problem, as opposed to applying a bandage to a symptom. Root cause analyses are discussed in more detail later in this chapter.

Document the Fix

Information on troubleshooting incidents needs to be stored in a central repository. This doesn't mean that we have to go nuts (though there are vendors who would be happy to sell us an expensive solution). In many environments, it is enough to have a shared directory with an appropriate subdirectory structure and file naming scheme.

A key document that needs to be included in this repository is a sign-off from the service owner agreeing that the problem has been resolved. This may seem like "administrivia," but the discipline of getting a sign-off ensures that we have understood and addressed the end-user complaint. It also ensures that the end-user spends the time to check it out (or at least takes some ownership for future occurrences of the problem). We don't have to write up a contract that requires approval from Legal. In many environments, a copy of a thank you email from the service owner is good enough.

At a bare minimum, the problem resolution documentation needs to include the following:

- Problem statement.

- Problem description documents, including dates and times of occurrences.

- Any vendor service order or correspondence associated with the problem.

- Information about the hypotheses generated during brainstorming, including any diagrams or documents used to organize them. (If a white-board discussion has been a central part of the process, take a digital photo of it and save it as part of the problem history.)

- Descriptions and results of testing. (This may be as simple as a checklist or a collection of saved emails.)

- A confirmation and acceptance document from the service owner.

At the very least, archive copies of the emails between members of the troubleshooting team. The key thing is that they be organized in a way that they can be found if we need to reference them in the future.

Over time, the collection of data on resolved problems can become a valuable resource. It can be referenced to deal with similar problems. It can be used to track recurring problems over time. Or it can be used to continue the troubleshooting process if it turns out that the problem was not really resolved after all.

CASE STUDY

Here is how we would apply these techniques to the familiar scenario of a system crash.

Soltest, a Solaris server, crashed on Thursday morning at 1:32 am. Fortunately, this system is part of a high-availability cluster of web servers, so services were not interrupted. We have the freedom to work on soltest immediately, rather than having to try to bring the system online by any means necessary to limp through to a maintenance window.

Problem Statement

Our problem statement in this case is very straightforward: "soltest panicked on Thursday morning at 1:32am." Note that this problem statement does not include any value judgments about difficulties caused by the system panic, it does not include any hypotheses as to the cause, and it does not include a list of immediately observable symptoms.

Problem Description

Our next task is to fully describe the problem by collecting as many symptoms as possible. We end up with the following:

A core file was generated by the system panic. A quick examination of the core file shows that httpd was active at the time of the panic.

POST reports "Hypertransport Sync Flood occurred on last boot." The vendor web site identifies this as a memory error.

BIOS and service processor System Event Log information report errors on the DIMM at CPU0, slot 1.

The fault LEDs are lit for CPU0, slots 0 and 1.

Identify Differences and Changes

Our records for the system show that memory was upgraded six months ago.

Brainstorm

The obvious conclusion is that the cause of the problem is a bad DIMM. Rather than jumping immediately to replacing the DIMM, we take the time to think through the Ishikawa diagram in Figure 9-4.

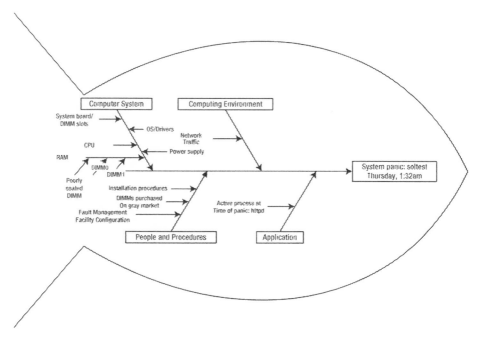

Figure 9-4. Ishikawa diagram: memory error

(Note that some of the items on the diagram are extremely low probability events. The purpose of a brainstorming exercise is to generate possible explanations, not to filter them. We want to encourage hare-brained speculation in this step. Sometimes those oddball hypotheses end up being the real cause or at least triggering a thought that leads to the root cause.)

Because we are disciplined enough to think through each aspect of the system, we make several interesting observations:

1. Experience has shown that sometimes an error reported on one DIMM is actually a result of a bad memory chip elsewhere in the same bank. Hardware manufacturers have gotten better at identifying the failing part, but we should consider the possibility that the other DIMM in the bank is the bad part.

2. The DIMM may be poorly seated, not failed. This can be due to a faulty slot on the system board, or it may be due to a poorly installed DIMM.

3. CPU or CPU cache errors sometimes manifest as "memory errors."

4. Could an OS or driver bug be at fault? We can certainly check SunSolve's bug database against our current patch level.

5. Bad power supplies can sometimes cause failures of other components.

6. Could high network traffic have caused the problem?

7. We sometimes purchase gray market DIMMs. Perhaps they sent us a bad part? Maybe we should be more careful about choosing our suppliers?

(Here, *gray market* refers to a legitimate but unapproved vendor who sells refurbished parts or new parts purchased through other than a manufacturer-approved VAR. Gray market parts may void your service contract or warranty. If you're dealing with parts that "fell off the back of a truck," you are dealing with black market parts, and you deserve whatever ill fortune comes your way. Shame on you.)

8. Can we configure the Fault Management Facility to handle memory errors more gracefully?

9. The httpd process was active at the time of the panic. Could this have generated the error?

Rank the Likely Causes

We have generated quite a few hypotheses. It makes sense to look for possible relationships to make sure that we examine any possible root causes.

In the real world, IDs are frequently generated by writing the various proposed causes on Post-It notes on a white board, then rearranging them and drawing relationship arrows between them. Working through this process in this case yields a few observations, which are illustrated in Figure 9-5.

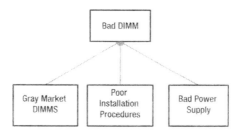

Figure 9-5. Memory error interrelationship diagram

One relationship that jumps out is the possibility that our purchasing policy (gray market DIMMs) may have led to an installation of a bad part. In this case, we have a possible ultimate cause (purchasing policy) and a possible proximate cause (bad DIMM) that both need to be examined.

Another possible relationship is that our installation procedure may have damaged a DIMM during the upgrade. In this scenario, our ultimate cause would be poor installation procedures and our proximate cause would be the resulting bad DIMM (Since the upgrade was six months ago, we can rank this as a low probability hypothesis.)

A bad power supply may have led to a failing DIMM.

High network traffic or some activity of httpd may have resulted in exercising the bad piece of memory, but they can't reasonably be considered to be the "cause" of the problem in any meaningful sense.

1. Based on this, the ranking of the most likely hypotheses are the following:

2. The DIMM in slot 1, CPU 0 is faulty. (The most obvious candidate is usually the right one.)

3. The DIMM in slot 0, CPU 0 is faulty.

4. The DIMMs in the bank are improperly seated or have a bad DIMM slot.

5. CPU 0 has a problem.

6. An OS or driver problem is improperly reporting a memory error.

In addition, we need to examine the possible ultimate causes of the gray market parts or the poor installation procedures. Both of these are possible problems with broad ramifications, and they should be examined.

Test the Hypotheses

The hardware vendor outlines a procedure for investigating memory errors in the diagnostics manual for these servers. When investigating a hardware error, we should always check vendor documentation for their recommendations about how to proceed with testing. Sometimes there are built-in testing facilities that we are unfamiliar with, and sometimes there are hardware-specific issues that we don't know about.

The vendor can recommend a procedure for identifying whether it is a bad DIMM, a mis-seated DIMM, a system board problem, or a CPU problem.

In addition to the fun with hardware, we need to take the time to examine the other two potential root causes. (We can do this while the memory stress test is running.)

We can examine the quality issues with our gray market vendor by looking at the repair history of parts purchased through them. We may also want to consider whether we may have voided service contracts or system warranties by purchasing nonapproved parts, and whether the extra costs and risks associated with our decision are justified by our cost savings.

And our installation procedures should be reviewed in any case. Everyone should be reminded to take proper antistatic and hygienic precautions (wash hands, clean work area, etc.) and to install parts in a manufacturer-approved manner.

The power supply should also be investigated, because power supply problems can be very difficult to track down. General practice is to start looking at the power supply as a possible culprit when there have been multiple part failures over a relatively short period of time. Unless there is actually a fault light on the power supply, it is difficult to pin down power supply problems, especially intermittent ones.

The steps outlined by the vendor can be very involved. In some cases, (with the concurrence of our service vendor, if any), it might make sense to shotgun the problem by replacing suspected parts one at a time. After each replacement, diagnostics (including a stress test) should be run. Parts removed during a shotgunning session should always be discarded, even if we don't think they are bad to avoid intermittent problems with that part in the future. The usual practice when shotgunning is to replace parts in order of cost (cheapest first), rather than likelihood. Individual cases may be handled differently.

Apply the Fix

In this case, our failed part has been replaced as part of our testing regime. The ultimate cause, however, may still be out there. Any changes to our purchasing and installation procedures also need to be implemented.

Verify the Fix

In this case, stress tests, are a good way to validate our fix. Procedural changes also need to be verified and approved by the relevant managers.

Document the Resolution

In some environments, it is enough to bundle together the logs and documents generated during the troubleshooting session and put them in a directory share with a defined structure. In this case, for example, perhaps we could create a directory for the soltest server, with a subdirectory named according to the date and a brief problem description (yyyymmdd-ProblemDescription). Our diagrams, notes, and emails can be saved to this directory. We should also include a document containing any service order numbers created with our service provider.

In larger environments, it may be worthwhile to set up a problem resolution database to allow searches of problem resolution information.

We also need to include a sign-off document from the system owner verifying that the problem is resolved.

Root Cause Analysis

Too often we see people who think that they have "fixed" the problem because the immediate emergency is over. In fact, people who don't resolve the root problem are condemned to a continual break/fix treadmill. The discipline of root cause analysis was invented to help us break the firefighting cycle and actually get the problem fixed for once and for all.

Systems administration is not the only discipline to have problems that need us to dig down to the ultimate causes. Fortunately, root cause analysis is general enough to be applied to a broad range of problems.

5 Whys

The simplest version of root cause analysis is sometimes called the "5 Whys" method developed by Toyota Motor Corporation. This method proposes that for most problems, by asking "why" a problem occurs, and asking "why" each successive explanation occurs, we can arrive at the root cause within 5 iterations. There is nothing magical about the number 5; the exercise should be repeated until we get to something that is recognizable as a root cause. Example 9-1 illustrates

---

EXAMPLE 9-1. 5 WHYS

Problem Statement: The system crashed. (Why?)

A memory chip failed. (Why?)

The machine room temperature exceeded recommendations. (Why?)

The HVAC unit is undersized given our heat load. (Why?)

Our projections for heat load were lower than what has been observed. (Why?)

We did the heat load projections ourselves rather than bringing in a qualified expert.

There are some serious weaknesses to the 5 Whys method:

- The results are not repeatable. We may well end up with different results depending on who runs the exercise. For example, what if we had answered the second "why" with some other plausible explanation—such as, "The chip was installed improperly" or "The manufacturer's quality control is inadequate"?

- We are limited to the participants' knowledge of the system. In particular, we aren't going to find any answers that the participants don't already suspect.

- We may not ask "why?" about the right symptoms of the problem.

- We may stop short and not proceed to the actual root cause of the problem. For example, people may stop at the point about the HVAC unit being undersized, run the estimates themselves, and promptly purchase a larger (but still undersized) unit.

These problems can be addressed, usually by reaching a group consensus about the appropriate answer for each "why" and by performing rigorous testing wherever possible.

Current Reality Tree

Eliyahu Goldratt presented a *Theory of Constraints* to resolve issues with organizational problem solving.[2] One of the cornerstones of the Theory of Constraints is a type of diagram known as a *Current Reality Tree* (CRT).

The Current Reality Tree has a number of similarities with the Interrelationship diagram. As with the ID, the CRT's primary components are boxes describing symptoms and arrows representing relationships between them. There are several key distinctions between an ID and a CRT:

- Arrows may flow in both directions if necessary. In particular, this allows us to identify a negative feedback loop.

- Symptoms are divided into undesirable effects (UDE) and neutral effects (NE). This allows us to recognize the effects of things in our environment that are not viewed as undesirable, but which may contribute to a UDE.

- Two or more symptoms may have their arrows combined with an ellipse. In a CRT, this means that the combination of those symptoms is sufficient to provoke the following UDE, but that all of them are required to ensure that the following UDE occurs. (In other words, the combination of UDEs and NEs is both necessary and sufficient to provoke the following UDE.)

- Because of the emphasis on identifying combinations of effects that are both necessary and sufficient, CRTs can sometimes flush out symptoms that are not obvious at first glance. As a result, CRTs can be better at getting to a real root cause than either Ishikawa diagrams or Interrelationship Diagrams (IDs).[3]

---

[2]Eliyahu M. Goldratt, *Essays on the Theory of Constraints*. Great Barrington, MA: North River Press, 1987.

[3]See Anthony Mark Doggett, "A Statistical Analysis of Three Root Cause Analysis Tools," *Journal of Industrial Technology* 20 (Feb.-April 2004): 5. www.nait.org/jit/Articles/doggett010504.pdf.

Building a CRT

Building a CRT has a lot in common with building Ishikawa and Interrelationship diagrams. First, we ask a key question with our Problem Statement. The question will usually be of the form "Why is this happening?" or "Why did this happen?"

Next, we need to create a list of several undesirable effects that are related to the key question. Each of these UDEs gets a box (or perhaps a Post-It note on a white board). These are arranged from top to bottom, where the top symptoms are the result of the symptoms from lower rows.

Wherever we can say something like "If A, then B," we would draw an arrow from A to B. Where we can say something like "If A is combined with B, then we get C," we would draw arrows from A and B to C, then group the arrows with an ellipse. (See Figure 9-6.)

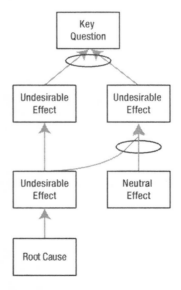

Figure 9-6. Basic current reality tree

We may also identify a feedback loop, where an effect has a direct impact on one of its own causes. Figure 9-7 illustrates such a loop.

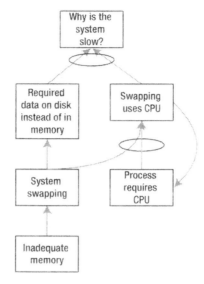

Figure 9-7. Feedback loop in a CRT

In Figure 9-7, we consider the case of a CPU-bound service on a system with inadequate memory. The system starts to swap, which slows down the process because data is stored in swap space rather than memory, and CPU resources are required to run the page scanner and perform swapping.

During this exercise, we may find it necessary to add more symptoms, either undesirable effects or neutral effects. We should not add UDEs or NEs that are not part of a key causality chain, or that are simply "facts of life." We want to try to keep the diagram clean enough that it can be used to spur thinking about how to resolve the root causes; it doesn't make sense to put in items that are tangential or environmental.

We will likely have two or more branches of the tree. Wherever possible, we should try to identify connections between the branches, such as symptoms that would cause the lowest-level effects of both branches.

At the lowest level of the CRT, we should ask "Why?" and continue to build the tree down until we are at the Root Causes, also known as *Problems*. If the lowest-level boxes are still just symptoms of an underlying problem, build down as far as possible by asking "Why?" at each stage.

It is possible to have more than one root cause for a problem. In this case, we would want to identify which of the causes is predominant. If one of the root causes is responsible for more than 70% of the UDEs, it is designated the *Core Problem*; it should receive our attention first. (Pareto diagrams, discussed in the final section of this chapter, may help us to identify the Core Problem.)

In Figure 9-8, for example, the Core Problem is that we have inadequate memory. We could argue that an alternative root cause is that we don't have enough CPU resources to swap efficiently, but a reasonable system administrator would have to admit that more than 70% of the problem is due to the memory shortage.

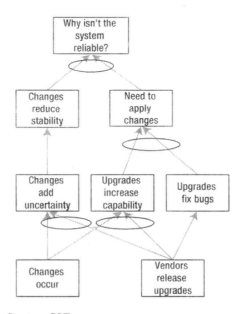

Figure 9-8. Core conflict in a CRT

It is also possible that at the lowest level, we will end up with a *Core Conflict* between two or more otherwise neutral effects. The combination of these two NEs, or the conflicts between them may end up causing the UDEs further up the diagram.

Evaporating Cloud

The *Evaporating Cloud* refers to Goldratt's method for dealing with conflicts. In particular, Goldratt discusses the *Core Conflict Cloud* representing the Core Conflict in our CRT.

The cloud metaphor describes the sense of unease we feel when faced with a seeming choice between two necessary conditions. Most of the time, we feel that we are caught in a situation where the best we can do is get away with some sort of unsatisfactory compromise.

In an Evaporating Cloud diagram, the end goal (aka the *Systemic Objective*) is placed in a box on the left. The two conflicting *Prerequisite Conditions* are placed in boxes at the right hand side of the drawing, with a lightning bolt arrow between them. The Necessary Conditions for the Systemic Objective are placed in boxes next to their respective conflicting prerequisite conditions. See Figure 9-9, for an example.

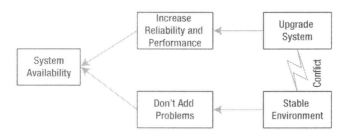

Figure 9-9. Evaporating cloud

Many conflicts can be resolved by defining the *Necessary Conditions* as narrowly as possible to reach the Systemic Objective, then seeing if this allows a redefinition of the *Prerequisite Conditions* that eliminates the conflict. The goal of a Theory of Constraints thinking exercise is to reach a win/win solution to a problem that leverages constraints rather than viewing them as obstacles.

Figure 9-9 illustrates the age-old conflict between upgrades and system stability. On the one hand, upgrades will increase the system reliability and performance. Neglecting upgrades for too long will eventually result in system problems. On the other hand, changes always carry some risk, so there is a strong desire to avoid the pain of changes, including upgrades.

In this case, we need to recognize the end goal of providing a reliable service. Upgrades need to be performed, but should be performed in a way that allows for adequate planning and testing to avoid introducing problems to a working system.

This sort of solution "evaporates" the cloud. In the Theory of Constraints, we can now build a *Future Reality Tree*, which is like a Current Reality Tree, except that it will represent the system with the changes we recommended to evaporate the cloud. These additional changes are called *injections*. Figure 9-10 includes an example of a Future Reality Tree with our injections.

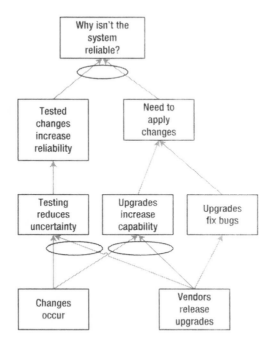

Figure 9-10. Future reality tree

Pareto Diagram

Pareto diagrams are designed to help us identify which of several items is responsible for most of the problems we face. The Pareto Principle is an observation that states that in many real-world cases, 80% of the problems come from 20% of the components.

We would create a Pareto diagram by identifying "buckets" of factors into which we will sort incidents. Each incident is assigned to only one bucket. Based on which buckets are responsible for the most incidents, we know where we should focus our efforts. In the case of buckets assigned to different root causes in a CRT, the Pareto diagram tells us which cause is the Core Problem.

In Figure 9-11, the numbers on the left side of the graph indicate the raw number of incidents associated with each bucket in the bar graph. The numbers on the right side indicate the cumulative percentage of incidents reflected by the buckets to the left of each point on the upper line graph.

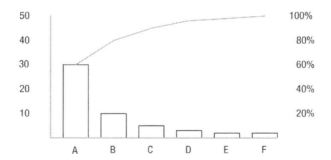

Figure 9-11. Pareto diagram

One way to interpret Figure 9-11 is that cleaning up cause A will eliminate 60% of the problem occurrences. Eliminating A and B will eliminate 80% of the incidents.

Analyses such as Pareto analysis are only possible if information on past incidents have been collected. This is an example of why it is so important to document incidents.

Summary

There are a number of tools available to assist in troubleshooting and root cause analysis exercises. Historically, these have been used more by business people, especially on production floors. But where these methods have been applied in IT settings, they have been successful in helping identify and resolve issues.

Discussion Questions

Think of a problem in your environment.

1.   Draw an Ishikawa diagram to help identify possible causes.

2.   Draw Interrelationship diagrams to help rank the most likely causes.

3.   Draw a Current Reality Tree showing the environment. Use an Evaporating Cloud to identify possible solutions.

4.   What possible resolutions have you found for the problem?

Further Reading

Cromar, Scott. "Troubleshooting Methods," *SysAdmin Magazine* 16, no. 8 (2007): 33–38.

Cromar, Scott. *Solaris Troubleshooting Handbook*. North Charleston, SC: CreateSpace, 2008.

Doggett, Anthony Mark. "A Statistical Analysis of Three Root Cause Analysis Tools." *Journal of Industrial Technology* 20, no. 2 (2004): 1–9, www.nait.org/jit/Articles/doggett010504.pdf.

Litt, Steve. "Shotgunning," *Troubleshooting Professional Magazine* 9, no. 4 (2005). www.troubleshooters.com/tpromag/200510/200510.htm.

Mizuno, Sigeru, ed. *Management for Quality Improvement: The Seven New QC Tools*. Cambridge: Productivity Press, 1988.

Mosley, Henry. *Current Reality Trees: An Action Learning Tool for Root Cause Analysis*. Baltimore, MD: Strategic Leadership Seminar for Population and Reproductive Health, 2006. www.jhuccp.org/training/scope/starguide/toc/rootcauseanalysis.ppt.

Ohno, Taiichi. *Toyota Production System: Beyond Large-Scale Production*. Portland, OR: Productivity Press, 1988.

Patrick, Francis S. *Taking Advantage of Resistance to Change (and the TOC Thinking Processes) to Improve Improvements*. Hillsborough, NJ: Focused Performance, 2001. www.focusedperformance.com/articles/resistanceslides.pdf.

Schwalbe, Kathy. *Information Technology Project Management*. Boston, MA: Thompson, 2006.

Shelford, Thomas J., and Gregory A. Remillard. *Real Web Project Management*. Boston, MA: Addison-Wesley, 2002.

U.S. Department of Energy. *DOE Guideline: Root Cause Analysis Guidance Document* (Report No. DOE–NE–STD–1004–92). Washington, DC: U.S. Department of Energy, Office of Nuclear Energy, 1992.

Youngman, Kelvyn. *A Guide to Implementing the Theory of Constraints (TOC)* website, 2007. www.dbrmfg.co.nz.

Influence Networks

Getting things done requires more than a position. You need respect, and sometimes you need friendship. Sometimes you need to be able to get things done without having the authority to make it happen.

Responsibility without Authority

In almost any environment, workers will find themselves in situations in which they are expected to produce results, even when not all of the factors are under their control. There are several different types of influence you might be able to exercise to get the job done:

- **Authority.** This is when you have direct hierarchical authority over the other person.

- **Assignment.** This is the extent to which you can affect the other person's future work assignments.

- **Budget.** The extent to which you can authorize (or get authorization for) discretionary expenditures.

- **Promotion.** The control or input you might have into the other person's potential promotions in the workplace.

- **Compensation.** Your influence into the other person's pay or benefits.

- **Penalty.** Your ability to cause the other person to be punished.

- **Challenging work.** Your ability to involve the other person in work perceived to be challenging or interesting.

- **Expertise.** Special expertise that you have that makes you attractive to work with.

- **Friendship.** Personal relations between you and the other person.

When H. J. Thamhain and D. L. Wilemon[1] investigated how effective these different methods were, they found that coercive methods (such as authority, assignment, compensation, or penalty) were much less effective than methods such as providing opportunities to learn through challenging, interesting work with people with a special expertise.

One thing to take away from this is that you don't need hierarchical authority to get things done. Engage people on a level other than the strictly hierarchical, and you may even get better results.

Reciprocity

Reciprocity is the understanding that when you do something for someone else, they "owe" you something of similar value. Usually, this is not stated quite so baldly in day-to-day interactions. (Sometimes it is, as when someone "calls in a favor.") Most of the time, people like to work in an environment where when they provide a useful service, the other person will eventually feel obligated to provide a service of similar value.

Note *80/20 rule:* 80% of the work is done by 20% of the people.

Corollary to the 80/20 rule: If you don't know who the 20% are, you are one of the 80%.

No influencing tactic will work unless the other person feels that they are getting some value from providing the service. It could be something concrete, in the form of an immediate tradeoff. It could be a feeling of worth and accomplishment from contributing to a larger success. Or it could be an obligation that can be called in later. ("I'll owe you one.")

When you develop a good working relationship with someone, it is full of little day-to-day reciprocities of different types. Eventually, you develop a trust relationship where you help each other out without even thinking about it or "keeping score," because you know that the other person is "good for it."

---

[1] Kathy Schwalbe. *Information Technology Project Management.* Boston, MA: Thompson, 2006.

Everyone Is a Potential Ally

When you run up against someone who is in your way, it is natural to think of that person as an adversary. If you turn it around and think of them as a potential ally, things change.

If you think of someone as an adversary, you lock down and become defensive. Rather than looking for ways to convince the other person to help you, you are more likely to try to use coercive means to get what you want.

Over the long haul, coercion does not work.

What Is It That You Want, Anyway?

An important part of getting what you need is to identify what your own needs and wants are. Which of those are actually necessary? And which of them are merely nice-to-haves? What is your bottom line?

Now, think about what the other person needs or wants. If you can provide them something of value, you are part of the way to setting up a relationship of reciprocity with them.

In IT, a lot of the things that we need are things that we will need again tomorrow, and the day after that. It is in your best interest to find a way to build a reciprocal relationship of trust with the other person.

What Do I Have to Trade?

There are a lot of different types of currencies that you may have access to when trying to build a reciprocal relationship:

- **Inspiration.** Don't underestimate the power of motivating someone to help you because it is the right thing to do. Explain why it is good for the organization, why it is the right thing to do, or why this task gives them a chance to demonstrate excellence.

- **Resources.** Perhaps your project has budget resources that can be assigned. Or maybe you have access to equipment, expertise, or space that the other person would find useful.

- **Learning opportunities.** Technology people value the chance to learn a new skill above almost everything else.

- **Faster response.** Can you arrange for something to be expedited for the other person?

- **Information.** Can you provide the other person with needed information?

- **Recognition.** It costs nothing to send an email to the person's boss explaining what an awesome job he or she did.

- **Visibility.** Is this something that management is watching?

- **Contacts.** Can the task lead to valued contacts with other people?

- **Team membership.** Perhaps the task is a way to become part of a successful team.

- **Relationship.** Don't underestimate the power of personal connections.

- **Ownership.** Can the other person be provided ownership of an important facility?

There also are negative currencies, many of which are withholding something from the above list. Wherever possible, lean to the positive.

The value of each of these currencies may be different from person to person. Try to select a currency that works for the person you are dealing with. Just because one particular currency is more valuable to you, that doesn't mean that the other person feels the same way.

Tenacity

Sometimes the key to getting things done is just not to give up.

Sometimes you will have to retrench or take a different tack to get where you need to go. Stay pleasant. Stay professional. Organize the facts, and make sure that the facts are on your side.

People will rethink their assumptions if you can approach things the right way. Sometimes you are turned down because it is easier to say no. Make it easier to say yes.

You may need to lobby decision makers one-on-one to get forward motion. When you do, present your case in a way that makes it easier for them to agree with you.

- **Find the places where you agree.** This may require some research on your part, but there are interests that the other person has that will be best served by moving forward.

- **Work past personality conflicts.** You may have a personality conflict with the other person, but don't let it become a contest. Everyone is best served by solving the problem. Make that your focus.

- **Think about areas where you can be flexible.** Demonstrating flexibility on noncore issues can make it easier for the other person to be flexible where it matters most for you.

- **Make sure you are talking to the decision maker.** If the other person is just reflecting a decision made by someone else, you need to find a way to speak with the decision maker.

- **Use an appropriate communication style.** Different people react differently to different communication styles. This can include things such as the mode of communication (email? phone? personal contact?) as well as the tone and the types and presentation of evidence that will be most convincing.

- **Which people are effective at implementing changes within the environment?** Can you emulate their approach? Or can you lobby some of them to help you?

- **Work out issues person-to-person.** When an issue is getting in the way, it is frequently more effective to negotiate a resolution one-on-one.

- **Hunt the other person down.** If you aren't getting a response, you may need to stake out someone's office or look for them in the break room. If it is important, find a way to have the conversation.

- **Lobby the people around the decision maker.** If you can win some of the decision-maker's allies to your point of view, it will make a difference.

If success was easy, everyone would be successful. If you want to be known as the manager who gets things done, be tenacious.

Managing Upward

When you are younger, it seems self-evident that people higher on the organizational chart have more freedom to make decisions. As you become more experienced, you start to see that everyone is constrained, just in different ways.

Part of being an effective manager is your ability to influence changes in a way that will benefit the overall organization. Sometimes you have a clearer view of the situation than someone higher in the organization, and you need to find a way to make a positive change take place.

Frequently you can make requests at the time that you and your manager set your goals. You can use that opportunity to adjust your boss's expectations if you can present a better alternative. You can also use that opportunity to explain to your boss what you need to achieve the goals being set for you.

Identify What You Need

Before making a request (especially a controversial request) of management, make sure you understand what you actually need.

- **Resources.** This can be something such as money, staff time, access to an expert, etc.

- **Authority.** Usually the authorization from upper management to make a key decision.

- **Influence.** This may be a request to weigh in on your behalf on a decision being made by someone else.

- **Advice or information.** Sometimes you need more information to make sure what you are doing is aligned with the organization's goals.

Try to understand what your core requirements are before you make your request. That way you will have room to negotiate and maybe bring up a new approach to achieve your end goal. Keep in mind that your ultimate goal is to move the organization forward, and that what you are requesting is just a means to that end.

Find an Approach

The first step is to identify who has the power to make the decision you need made. Then decide what type of approaches might be successful.

What is the decision-maker's perspective? Try to think through the priorities and viewpoints that might be relevant to the decision you need made.

Are there people that the decision maker trusts and respects? You may be able to ask them for help. This is not deceptive or manipulative. Keep in mind that your motivation is what is best for the organization. The decision-maker's allies may be able to provide some insight about how best to pitch your proposal, and what priorities should be emphasized. They also may help you tweak your proposal to make it more likely to succeed.

If the decision maker is a group, tackle the people in that group. Figure out what motivates them and what concerns they are likely to raise. Most concerns and objections to your proposal are entirely predictable; make sure that you have answers that will resonate with the people in the group.

Sometimes you may need to divide your proposal into pieces to make each part more palatable, or to make the parts fit into the organizational structure better. If you do that, make sure the parts will be able to stand on their own as well as part of a larger proposal.

Some common approaches are

- **Direct approach**. Ask the decision maker directly for what you need.

- **Conversation**. If you and someone else are competing for a resource or have incompatible ideas about how to proceed that you can't resolve, ask the decision maker to meet with the two of you to negotiate a resolution.

- **Use influence**. You can use your influence to have other people express support for your proposal or even propose it directly themselves.

- **Group meeting**. Group meetings can be unpredictable. Try to get a line on the views of the other people in the meeting, including objections they might raise. The better you prepare, the more likely you will be successful.

You might have to mix and match these approaches. And you might be turned down and need to recast your proposal in a way that is more likely to be successful. Frequently a rejection will include information that you were not aware of. Sometimes this information will make you rethink your proposal or come up with a way to deal with the new information.

However things work out, make sure to ask yourself honestly what your motivations are. As long as you are working for the best interest of the organization, keep looking for a way to help the organization improve.

HOW TO BE A GOOD TEAMMATE

Treat other people right. When people come to you for help with a proposal that has merit, see if you can help them.

Shield your subordinates from unreasonable requests, but make sure that your team is doing everything it can to improve the organization's position in the competitive landscape.

Encourage your subordinates and peers. Celebrate their accomplishments. Just like you want to be recognized for your good work, make sure to recognize the people around you.

Stay positive. When there are problems, be the person who looks for a solution. Technical people love to solve puzzles. The world is full of puzzles; enjoy them.

Communicate. Make sure that people around you know what you are doing, and why you are doing it. Make them aware of what you will need from them in advance, and ask them what they will need from you going forward.

Summary

You will frequently face situations where you are responsible, but where you do not directly control the resources needed to succeed. Part of being an effective leader is being able to work with other people in the environment to accomplish your goals.

Discussion Questions

1. Is there someone who is effective in your environment? Which tactics does this person use to engage other people?

2. Which resources do you need that you do not control? Who controls those resources? What will be the most effective way to approach that person?

Further Reading

Berkun, Scott. *Making Things Happen*. Sebastopol, CA: O'Reilly, 2008.

Cohen, Allan R., and David L. Bradford. *Influence without Authority*, 2nd ed. Hoboken, NJ: Wiley, 2005.

Harvard Business Essentials. *Manager's Toolkit*. Boston, MA: Harvard Business School Press, 2004.

Schwalbe, Kathy. *Information Technology Project Management*. Boston, MA: Thompson, 2006.

Watkins, Michael. *The First 90 Days*. Boston, MA: Harvard Business School Press, 2003.

Managing a Dispersed Team

Geographically dispersed teams have become a reality in most large workplaces. Organizations pressed to reduce costs are shifting work from high-cost locations to lower-cost locations.

This is a politically fraught question, for all sorts of obvious reasons. I'm not going to address the political issues; that is a topic covered exhaustively by a lot of other books. This book is about challenges faced by managers, and this chapter will be focused on that.

■ **Note**   *Outsourcing* is when work that was previously done in-house is done by an employee of a different company.

Offshoring is when work previously done in one country is moved to people in another country.

Nearshoring is a type of offshoring that uses people in nearby time zones to increase overlap between peoples' work schedules.

The challenges for dealing with all these types of team distributions are similar. In all cases, you are communicating and trying to forge a cohesive team across boundaries of space, time, and culture.

Outsourcing and offshoring have caused a tremendous change in the way that information technology work is done. Coordination must be done across geographical and organizational boundaries. Cultural differences between people in different companies, regions, and countries have to be overcome. The challenges faced by IT managers today are different in scope and flavor from the challenges that were faced by previous generations.

The most difficult challenge is making a team out of this diverse group of people, separated by language, geography, time zone, and culture.

Is Offshoring More Efficient?

A lot of the analysis done by companies focuses strictly on the cost of salaries and benefits for comparable professionals in different locations. This sort of analysis is naïve and incomplete.

There are increased transaction and efficiency costs associated with both offshoring and outsourcing. These include increased travel and communication costs associated with managing the remote team members, as well as risk mitigation costs associated with doing business in a country with a different regulatory structure. In some cases, companies have found that these additional costs outweigh the savings in salaries and benefits, and they are reversing the process (commonly known as *onshoring* or *insourcing*.)

Advantages and Risks of Global Teams

Executive management tends to overstate the economic benefits associated with offshoring to lower-cost locations. To someone who is not directly on the firing line, one system administrator looks like another system administrator, and the primary difference is the salary.

For people who have spent their careers managing technology directly, this type of thinking glosses over a lot of the bigger issues. There are a lot of advantages to having the technology staff closer to their internal customers.

- **Communications efficiency.** In-person communication is simply more efficient than remote communication. Eighty percent of the content of a conversation is nonverbal. Video conferencing and telephones allow some of the nuanced nonverbal information to come through but not all of it. Some functions, such as requirements gathering, are much more efficiently gathered face-to-face.

- **Ease of coordination.** Informal conversations allow back-channel communications to occur that can improve efficiency. It is much easier to request a small clarification, or for an improvement to come out of a quick conversation.

When you are in a different time zone than the requester, where you lose a business day to ask a question, you are more likely to just proceed based on your best judgment.

- **Local control.** It is never as easy to manage people remotely as locally. Management by walking around becomes impossible when you manage people in remote locations.

- **Cultural norms.** Cultural differences are less likely to garble communications or implicit assumptions about requirements.

- **Cohesion.** A sense of teamwork is easier to foster when people are closer together.

- **Local responsiveness.** It is easier to perform trouble-shooting and product enhancement exercises with local people.

- **Uneven workload expectations.** If all the escalations go to the remaining small group of employees at the home office, those people end up having to resolve all of the hard problems with a reduced staff.

- **Loss of core competencies.** If outsourcing is done too aggressively, an organization runs the risk of giving away its strategic advantage to a competitor or supplier, rather than bidding out commodity work. Managers need to have an understanding of which functions are strategic advantages to the organization, and which tasks can be outsourced without losing a core competency.

Having said that, there are some legitimate advantages to dispersing the team globally:

- **Avoid groupthink.** People from different locations and cultures bring different assumptions to the table. This can help avoid groupthink, as assumptions are challenged by having a more diverse group of team members.

- **Standardized, documented processes.** Pressure increases to improve documentation of procedures. This can result in lowered defect rates if handled properly.

- **More work hours in a day.** "Follow the sun" scheduling has the potential to allow teammates to have better work life balance. Once processes are set up, and a culture of trust is in place, project teams can continue to work problems around the clock.

Agreements to outsource or offshore functions usually include stringent SLAs (Service Level Agreements), which are going to have to be met. If you can get the distributed parts of your team working together smoothly, it will make a big difference in your ability to comply with your SLAs.

Time and Distance

Coordinating efforts across time zone boundaries can be difficult. Communications and responses are delayed. IT people are used to being able to ask clarifying questions to nail down requirements. But with time zone differences, a few rounds of clarifying questions and waiting for answers can mean delays of days or weeks.

In the next the following sections, I discuss several techniques that can help reduce the impact of this problem:

- Create a project rhythm.

- Set an expectation of synchronization.

- Create a place for people to introduce themselves.

- Collaborative technologies.

- Standardize the format for common requests.

- Standardize the process used to execute common requests.

- Have some team members adjust their schedules to overlap. These employees can bridge information to the rest of the team.

- Schedule team status meetings with team members from different regions.

- Schedule travel to remote locations to allow in-person contact.

- Celebrate accomplishments.

Project Rhythm

You won't have the advantage of the natural rhythms of meal and break times when you are dealing with remote team members. Artificial rhythms will need to be built into project schedules and team formalisms such as staff meetings. Create a place where it is natural for your team members to collaborate. Chat rooms, conference bridges, scheduled calls, and project milestones are all tools that you can use to create these rhythms.

Synchronization

Your team members need to learn that you expect them to synchronize regularly with their remote colleagues. Ask explicit questions about what the conversation was like the last time they touched base. You may need to ask to be cc'd on emails initially so that you can make sure your team members are getting into the habit of synchronizing with remote team members regularly.

Introductions

Team members need a space where they can express their individuality to the rest of the team. Social media tools offer a number of different ways for people to create profiles or personal summaries that other team members can view.

These introductions should include information about team members' professional histories and expertise. That way people know who might be able to help them with a question they have about the xyz protocol.

You do have to keep an eye on how much time is spent on this social media. As with a lot of things in life, there is a balance between making use of the tool and wasting project time.

Collaborative Technologies

There are quite a few technologies available to make it easier to collaborate over distance:

- Email.
- Voice mail (or video mail).
- Discussion groups.
- Groupware packages. (These allow collaborative authoring.)
- Revision control.
- Ticketing systems.
- Workflow tools.
- Whiteboarding and desktop sharing. (These frequently have a facility to record sessions for people in other time zones.)
- Calendaring and scheduling applications.

Richer applications, such as video conferencing, allow for a broader bandwidth communication, but at the cost of additional time and effort. The appropriate technology needs to be matched to the goal behind the communication.

Standard Formats for Requests

For common requests, your team members probably find themselves asking for the same information over and over. Generate a template that requesters need to fill out for these types of requests. This may be a web form, it could be a questionnaire, or it could be a spreadsheet. When a request arrives without the template information, push it back to the requester to fill out the form.

Compliance benefits everyone: the requesters are more likely to get what they want faster; your team is able to get its work done better; and the defect rate drops way down. Mention these benefits to your peers in the requesting teams when you introduce these templates; there is no reason you should not be able to get buy-in as long as your template is reasonable.

- **Ask for exactly what you need.** Questions may need to be reworked a few times until the customer base understands them.

- **Get feedback from your customer community on the initial drafts of the template.** Clarify points that need clarifying.

- **Do not ask for information that the customer is unlikely to have.** If it is information that your team can figure out, find a way to script or standardize that process to reduce the time and effort your team spends on research while also reducing the defect rate.

Standard Processes

If the team becomes disciplined about using standard processes, it will be easier for tasks to be handed back and forth between team members in different time zones. For example, if Fred in the United States is building a system, he can tell Samir in India that he is up to step 16 in the standard build process, and he can point him at the system request template for the needed information. After his shift, Samir can hand the build back to Fred for completion, and let him know that he is up to step 23.

It can take a while to get all the common processes documented and standardized. This is a lot of work, so team members will need to see some early wins to see the benefits of organizing things this way. Pick some early win processes to be documented and standardized. Ideally, these should have the following characteristics:

- Common requests are going to give the most return on the investment of time and effort.

- The requests need to have a lot of commonality in how they would be executed. If they do not, you need to rethink how you are characterizing requests.

- If you have a good procedure in place already, that will save some of the up-front preparation time.

- Multistep procedures are the easiest to transfer across time zones.

If people are resistant to transferring tickets midexecution, it may take some extra sales and mentoring time on your part to get things jumpstarted. Once it gets going, team members will start to see the benefits for themselves.

- They don't have to stay late as often to finish a high-priority request; the ticket can be completed by someone on the next shift.

- Issues get resolved quicker, which makes the requesters happier.

- It demonstrates the value of the team members in all the different regions. This helps deal with questions about whether the rest of the jobs are going to be offshored.

Make sure that the master company retains control and ownership of these standard operating procedures. In the event that a contract with an outsourcer comes to an end, the last thing the organization needs is to have to redraft operating procedures at the same time a team transition is taking place.

Bridge Schedules

Some team members can be allowed to move their schedules earlier or later in the day to overlap with their colleagues in other time zones. This overlap allows more time for communications and handovers. It helps avoid the problem with questions not being able to be answered until the beginning of the next shift.

Bridge employees also help build trust relationships between people in the different regions. Having familiar people in the other locations helps to break down cultural barriers, and it helps to create a dynamic of trust and teamwork across the different employee populations.

Team Meetings

Staff meetings across the regions allow team members to see what other team members are doing. This helps reduce resentments about work load, and it can help bring different perspectives to bear on common problems.

These will need to be scheduled at the beginning of one team's work day and at the end of another team's shift. There is no convenient way to schedule them; everyone will need to give a little for these to work.

Travel

Because the reasons for offshoring and outsourcing are frequently to achieve cost savings, it may be difficult to get a travel budget, and you will lose time when you are travelling. Even with all that, there is no real replacement for face-to-face contact when building a team.

Celebrate Accomplishments

Your team will really come together when they see substantive things that were accomplished by the team. Technical people like to get things done. When they succeed, find ways of celebrating. Here are a few ideas:

- A congratulatory email from someone high up the organization's food chain.

- Individual awards or certificates for each person's part in the project.

- A web page touting the accomplishment to the world, with specifics.

- Arrange for an edible treat to be delivered to team members in each site on the same day.

Cultural Differences

Language and cultural differences can interfere with how effectively a team is able to work together. Misunderstandings can sap a team's energy.

Different people from different cultures communicate in radically different ways. These are not always clear to people who are not used to working with people from the other countries in question.

These differences include differences in etiquette (dos and don'ts), values, beliefs, patterns of thinking, patterns of communication, among others.

It is easy to find lists of these differences. Here are a few frequently observed differences between Indian workers and their western colleagues:

- Indians engage in small talk less easily than their western counterparts. In some cases, technical training courses actually discourage students from engaging in small talk to avoid embarrassing exchanges.

- Inquiries about time schedules get different responses from different cultures. Indian respondents typically do not include time to deal with any difficulties. Managers can work around this by probing to find out which if any projected issues have been included in the time estimate.

- People from the southern part of India use what is sometimes called the "Indian wiggle" in which the head is shaken side to side. This is frequently misinterpreted by westerners as indicating "no" (i.e., as in a western "head shake"), when it really indicates anything from "I agree" to "I hear you."

- Indians frequently use a "wobbly yes" rather than saying "no." Western managers need to watch for a less-than-firm "yes" and drill down if necessary.

All of these are examples of differences in cultural norms. Unfortunately, it is all too easy to fall into the pattern of expecting that everyone else communicates the same way you do—after all, isn't that what makes "sense?"

There are no rights and wrongs here, just differences. Managers need to learn to understand and value different team members from different cultures. And they need to set a tone within the group where people are not meant to feel badly about who they are or where they live. Folks are just folks. Technical people are, by and large, hard-working, dedicated people. It is not easy for anyone to achieve technical competence. Value your people, no matter what their background is.

Cultural Orientations

There have been several different efforts to characterize cultural differences in measurable ways. One of the more effective ways of breaking things down was put forward by Geert Hofstede[1] and Edward Hall.[2] Some of the axes of cultural orientation that they proposed include the following:

---

[1] Geert Hofstede, *Culture's Consequences: Comparing Values, Behaviors, Institutions, and Organizations Across Nations* (Beverly Hills, CA: Sage Publications, 2001).
[2] Edward T. Hall, *Beyond Culture* (Garden City, NJ: Doubleday, 1976).

- **Power orientation.** This refers to the emotional distance between subordinates and superiors. Most Asian cultures and Russia tend to have more autocratic leadership cultures, while the United States, Israel, and most European countries tend toward more participatory cultures. When working across these cultural norms, someone from a more participatory culture may need to put forward extra effort to get input or constructive criticism from someone whose cultural leadership norm is less participatory.

- **Relationship orientation.** This can be expressed as individualism vs. collectivism. In general, wealthier cultures tend to be more individualistic than less wealthy cultures. This is true even within specific countries or even regions of particular countries. Managers need to be particularly sensitive when criticizing employees in a group. Reprimands should be handled individually.

- **Uncertainty orientation.** This axis has to do with a comfort with ambiguity, and a preference for rules and expectations to be set out explicitly.

- **Future orientation.** Cultures with a high future orientation value delaying gratification to improve the situation in the future. East Asian cultures, such as China, Japan, and Korea all have very high future orientation scores.

- **Communication orientation.** Low-context cultures listen more to what is said rather than considering the tonal and peripheral information about the communication. High-context cultures like to consider the context of a communication, which may not be apparent in an email. Northern European and US cultures are generally considered low-context cultures, whereas southern European, Latin American, and Asian cultures are high-context cultures.

- **Destiny orientation.** This is sometimes called fatalism, and reflects the extent to which someone believes they can control the future.

- **Universalist orientation.** This is the extent to which people believe that the same rules apply to everyone.

- **Information processing orientation.** Richard Nisbett performed research showing that Asians are more likely to see relationships and context, while westerners are more likely to see categories and taxonomies.[3] Different people are going to see the same situation differently.

These observations are generalizations, of course. Any time you are dealing with human beings, you need to get to know them as individuals to understand how they think and how they will react. But the cultural orientation axes are useful to help you think about how people are different, and how best to communicate with different people.

Language Differences

Even when English is used as the standard language, there are significant differences between how people from different cultures will understand the same set of English words.

Sometimes, this is a result of how the English word translates back to the speaker's native language. Sometimes, it is a result of words having a different connotation in different places. For example, the word *contractor* can be understood in India to mean a janitor, and a *vendor* is someone who sells things in the market. *Consultant* is a more appropriate word to use in India for someone who is providing services to your team.

For another example, consider what someone from Latin America means when they say *now*. Depending on the context, it may mean right away, or it could mean by the end of the business day. Spanish has more than one word that translates to *now*, so this is not a matter of a cultural difference so much as an incorrect translation of intent.

Beyond what words mean, many Americans have difficulty understanding accents of people from other countries, even of native English speakers from countries like India. Written communications can help bridge the gap while the American ear becomes accustomed to the different accent.

The key is to keep communications simple:

- Avoid slang and idioms. Use international English, with no sports metaphors.

- Be aware of words that may have different meanings for different cultures.

- Be explicit about expectations. State requirements and dates clearly and concisely.

---

[3]Richard E. Nisbett, *The Geography of Thought: How Asians and Westerners Think Differently, and Why* (New York, NY: Free Press, 2003).

- Break up long messages into paragraphs and bullet points. Keep sentences short and simple.

- Repeat urgent requests through multiple channels (e.g., email and phone conference).

- Request feedback to try to track down questions.

- Follow up verbal requests with something in writing.

Above all, clarify and follow up. Even when you think something is clear, it may not be understood on the receiving end.

Summary

There are few things as rewarding as coming to understand how people in another culture live their lives. Being able to manage people from another cultural background is challenging, but it can open up new ways for you to understand yourself.

Whether you are managing people from another culture, another time zone, or another city, the key will be clear and constant communication. When you manage a team that is all local, you get used to managing by walking around. When you manage a distributed team, get used to managing by communicating clearly, concisely, and repeatedly.

Discussion Questions

1. What information will an offshore team member need as part of your most frequent service requests? What are some options for communicating this information to the offshore team member?

2. One advantage of global teams is that support can be on a hand-off basis rather than an on-call basis. Which activities can be supported by an offshore team member?

Further Reading

Carmel, Erran, and Paul Tjia. *Offshoring Information Technology*. Cambridge: UK: Cambridge University Press, 2005.

Hofstede, Geert. Cultural Constraints in Management Theories. *Academy of Management Executive*, 7 no. 1 (1993): 81–93.

Nisbett, Robert E. *The Geography of Thought: How Asians and Westerners Think Differently, and Why*. New York, NY: Free Press, 2003.

Managing Software Development Teams

In most ways, managing a software team is just like managing any other type of technical team. Technical teams are all made of talented experts. The manager's job is to enable these experts to improve the organization's business capability.

But managing a software development team is also different than managing another type of team. Tools change and languages change, but software development is a profoundly creative enterprise. The widgets, libraries, and other primitives grow in size and complexity, but there are a nearly infinite number of possible ways to accomplish a particular task. A member of a software development team can put a personal stamp on his or her contribution in a way that most other technical people can't.

▓ **Note** A *primitive* is one of the basic building blocks that is assembled into a program.

This chapter is coauthored by David M. Jacobs.

With that nearly infinite number of ways to get from A to B comes a need for judgment and intuition. A good programmer will consistently identify efficient and easily communicated ways to accomplish a given task with the tools at hand.

It is probably impossible to come up with a definitive procedure for producing good code. That is why writing code is a human enterprise, and the talented humans who write code need both skill and intuition to do it well.

Code Quality

Defensive coding should be your foundation. Good programs should be resilient, easy to troubleshoot, and allow for graceful recovery from errors.

Fault-tolerant code will anticipate the possibility of problems, and will recover without causing data corruption. Error handling is an under-appreciated, critical part of good coding practices.

When evaluating your team members' work product, emphasize error handling, logging, and recoverability. As with any other value that you define as being important for your team, message relentlessly. Recognize excellence. Require dependability. If you measure and reward reliability, your team will produce reliable software.

Software Maintenance

Software that is big enough to really be useful is seldom written by one programmer. Most software is a collaboration across people and across time. As new capabilities are added or bugs fixed, new code is incorporated into a software package.

Maintaining software written by someone else is not usually a programmer's favorite task, but it has to be done. The same discipline and attention to detail that goes into a new development project has to be applied to software maintenance.

If your software development team understands the importance of maintainability, they will implement it. Make sure that they think of the development not as just a cool technical puzzle to solve, but as writing a block of code that can stand for generations.

Use code reviews and other techniques to make sure that the code coming from your team is clean, well-structured, and easily understood. That may mean in-line comments, or it may mean external documentation. Whatever method you use, make sure that your team's code will live well past the time when the team members have moved on to their next big jobs.

Maintainable code can achieve its own sort of immortality. If code is maintainable, the business has an incentive to keep the existing package (with enhancements) rather than undergo a painful migration. Help your developers develop a vision of their software as something that will help solve problems that they haven't even thought about yet. And then help them to follow disciplined documentation and structural practices that will help them achieve that goal.

Operational Excellence

If software is not written with operations in mind, it will fail in its primary mission: bringing value to the organization. Finicky, unreliable software consumes operational resources, creates resentments, and destroys the reputation of a software development group.

Operational excellence is built on attention to detail. Little things, such as disk housekeeping, log rotation, configurability, and security of temporary files all are hallmarks of excellent software. It doesn't take that much extra effort to be thoughtful. But the payoffs to the organization can be huge. And what helps the organization helps the development team.

Continuity

When designing software, consider how it will operate in a disaster recovery context. If the software cannot recover gracefully in your organization's business continuity environment, it will be a liability to the organization's disaster readiness.

How well does the code deal with an interruption in the plumbing connections to the database and other programs? How difficult is it to point it to new data sources in a new context, such as a disaster recovery?

If continuity is not built in at the beginning, the code will be a monster to recover. Nobody appreciates spending time and money developing an infrastructure to recover an application that was not developed with continuity in mind.

Scheduling

Your team's software also needs to be able to operate in the context of your organization's job scheduling environment.

Environment-variable settings should be addressed within the program context, from configuration files, rather than requiring that the execution environment have certain variables set in certain ways.

Status codes should be clearly defined and discrete so that the scheduler can branch execution paths depending on the outcome of the program.

It all boils down to understanding your team's code in a broader environmental context, rather than focusing on a narrow piece of functionality.

Software Reusability

Another type of software immortality is reuse. If a module is useful, well-documented, and maintainable, why write another module that does the same thing?

Objects created by developers should be organized into libraries that can be tapped by other developers. Recognize the tool builders within your team for the valuable contributions they make. And also recognize the people who increase the efficiency and velocity of your development process by reusing code from the repository.

Obviously, not every piece of code is suitable for reuse. Some problems are too specific for their solution to usefully be applied elsewhere. Experienced developers should be able to identify modules that are suitable for sharing in the repository.

There are some obvious obstacles to implementing an infrastructure that supports code reuse:

- Organizing the repository in a way that will be useful is nontrivial.

- The code in the repository needs to be maintained as bugs are fixed.

- The mind-set of the developers needs to be changed to look in the repository.

- There needs to be enough useful material in the repository for developers to have an incentive to look there.

- The organization's development mind-set needs to become more product centric and less project centric.

These obstacles are significant, and that is why so few companies have an organized code reuse system. Especially in organizations where project managers are brought on for a short-term project, there is little incentive for a project manager to invest resources from a limited budget into a code repository that will mostly benefit other project managers in the future.

If your organization hires project managers on a per-project basis, someone outside the project management infrastructure may need to take on the challenge of making the changes necessary to encourage code reuse.

Project Management Challenges

A common challenge for software development managers is that they need to pull in team members who actually report to someone else. There are some challenges involved with managing a team whose members' primary loyalty is to someone else.

When you don't have direct executive authority over someone, you still have a lot of things that you can offer as a project manager.

- Access to new technologies.

- The excitement of being part of a team making something new.

- Leadership opportunities within the project team.

- Project work looks good on resumes. Especially if it comes with a good recommendation from a project manager.

- A chance to get away from the daily grind.

Obviously, everything gets harder if the team member's regular manager is not enthusiastic about his or her participation. You may need to exercise some of the skills we discussed in Chapter 10 to encourage the manager to see the importance of the project. Or you may need to engage the project champion to reinforce the priority of the project.

Keep in mind that your project schedule depends on the availability of the resources you demanded when your project schedule was approved. If the resources available to you change, that also will mean that your project schedule is impacted. Make sure that this message is passed along to the project sponsors so that they understand how important it is to reinforce your authority over the resources you have been promised.

Scope Creep

In Chapter 4, we discussed the importance of battling scope creep. For software projects, scope creep is especially dangerous.

Maybe the nature of creating something out of nothing excites people and fires their imagination. Maybe the inputs are largely invisible to the end-user, so they assume that their requests are cheap. Whatever the reason, scope creep will strangle your software project if you don't tame the monster first.

Change management is your friend. Establish a process to examine the cost of every change before it is considered for approval. Cost may come as time, it may come as money, and usually it comes as both. If costs are inflexible (as they usually are), approvals may require a trade-off of another requirement.

Let your change management process work for you to let the ideas compete against each other.

You also can use the promise of the next version to put off requests that threaten your project. Suggestions that don't make it into the current release can be considered for the next release. When the time comes to scope out the next release, make sure to take a hard-eyed look at the accumulated suggestions. Some of them will be gold; some will be junk. Make sure to select requirements based on merit, not the length of time they have spent in the queue.

Explaining Complexity

A common problem is that people think that a feature that is easy to describe is easy to implement. This is obviously not true. It is nice to have a clear statement of a requirement, but that doesn't mean that the feature is easily implemented.

Sometimes complexity can be explained by showing the design that will be necessary to implement the feature. It is management's job to push on you to make sure the company's resources are not being wasted by too relaxed a project schedule. It is your job to push back with information and facts to demonstrate that you are making wise use of your project budget.

Some of the graphical tools discussed in Chapter 13 can help describe the magnitude of some of the changes that are being requested. You'll have to hold your ground against "simple" changes that threaten to derail the entire effort due to hidden complexity. Expose the complexity to the Change Control Board, and describe the costs of the change request accurately, in time, resources, and money.

The Importance of Testing

When people want to push a schedule, the first place that is considered for cuts is testing. Professionals understand just how important it is to have a complete test cycle. Issues are much more easily addressed when they are discovered during testing than if they are only discovered after the product's release into production.

Your team may also be a part of this dynamic. Programming tends to attract personalities who are eager to move on to the next challenge, not look back to fix minor errors in what they did yesterday. Preach the importance of quality within your team, and the importance of testing to achieving that quality.

Leave adequate time for testing. Push back on management or even your own team when necessary. If a schedule change is needed, it would be better to postpone a feature or bring on more people than to eliminate testing.

Testing As a Way to Measure Quality

One of the main benefits of a good testing program is that it will provide a solid quality metric. Once you get a handle on which team members need help to meet your quality goals, you will know where to focus your time and efforts.

As with many other things in the workplace, you get more of what you measure. If you measure quality, you will get more quality.

Every Requirement Gets a Test Suite

Every listed requirement needs a defined test suite to verify that the end product meets the requirement. Some methodologies even specify requirements in terms of the tests that are used to validate them.

Software engineering maps user requirements to functional requirements to code to tests. Every line of code should be able to be mapped back to the user requirements that demand it, as well as being able to be mapped forward to the test suites that validate those user requirements.

Team Motivation

Programmers are optimistic people. They need to be that way to believe that they can create something out of nothing. Software developers believe that what they write works, otherwise they would never have written it.

Just as management can sabotage a testing program by starving it of time and resources, developers can kill a testing program by neglect.

The importance of thorough testing needs to become engraved in your team's DNA. Testing is part of your overall emphasis on quality from start to finish. Poorly written tests are a sign of laziness or inattention. Mentor team members who tend to be more prone to skipping "unneeded" testing. Teach them how to test thoroughly, and then measure their quality directly. Pride is a powerful motivator, and measuring and recording defects will encourage more careful testing during the development process.

Business Value

Many other technology teams manage or build tangible capital assets. Unfair it may be, but senior management can view their contribution as being more valuable than a software team's contributions because it is easier to list those contributions on a balance sheet.

A software team's contributions are only valuable if they deliver more tangible value to the organization than the cost of running the team. Make sure that you have a business case to support your activities. Then make sure your business cases are in a well-publicized share that is available to management.

Document Your Progress

Unlike your peers in other technology areas, the products of a software development team are not visible until they are available for testing. For management, a software development team looks like a black box that consumes cash with no tangible output.

Make sure that management understands your project plan, and that they have a way to measure your progress toward completion. Communicate out your testing results, for unit tests, integration tests, and acceptance tests. These test results can be a way to demonstrate tangible progress toward the end goal.

For projects using prototyping methodologies, prototypes can also be tangible reminders to the project sponsors of why they are spending money on the project. One of the advantages of prototyping models is that management is less likely to lose faith in the project because they have a way to view tangible work products that show a clear progression toward the project goals.

Tool Selection

If your team is using a diverse set of tools, team members will not be able to help each other out when questions about those tools arise. And when they are troubleshooting a problem, it may be harder for different team members to reproduce the problem in the same way.

There is always some space for personal preference, but a software development team needs to be using a standard tool set. If one does not exist for your organization, part of your challenge will be to define one for your team.

Make sure to get the best tools you can arrange. Cost is always an issue, but skimping on tools is a false efficiency. Figure out how much more quickly your people can work on good tools versus crappy tools, and figure how much it will cost the company to have the software delivered that much later.

As with any other management challenge, discuss the issue with your team. Explain the problems that can arise from having different people using different tool sets. Foster a discussion of the pros and cons of the different tool choices. Then make a decision what the standard will be and get on with building the piece of software.

Repeatable Processes

There are some processes that you will revisit over and over throughout the development process. Code builds, deployments to a higher environment, database refreshes, and ETL (Extract, Transform, Load) tests are all examples of such processes. These should be handled in a defined, repeatable way.

If you take the time and thought to build the tools to support these processes, it will save you time on any project of significant size. If you look at the amount of time to do a database refresh, multiply by the number of times you have to do it, and then multiply by the number of developers idled by a database refresh, you will understand just how much it is worth your while to nail these processes down.

And if you can script and standardize your code deployment process, you will eliminate entire classes of problems, such as the problems caused by failing to upgrade a single module during the upgrade process.

Naming Conventions

If you don't have a standard naming convention for objects, you are likely to end up with multiple distinct objects having the same name, or with team members spending more time than you would like trying to resolve problems resulting from an incompatible naming scheme.

Come up with a standard and conventions. Circulate these for feedback from the project team, and take the feedback into account. Then publish the naming standard and insist on its use.

Backups and Version Control

Define a version control standard, and make sure there is a way to roll back to a previous version when a new bug is accidentally introduced in a new version. If there is an organizational standard for these capabilities, use that. But don't let the project get underway without these capabilities being used by your development team.

Bug Tracking System

Track bugs and reported issues in a standard, shared way. People on the project need to be able to examine bug reports and resolutions. It is your job to make sure that they have a standard tool and process for reporting and tracking bugs and issues.

Methodology

There are a ton of software methodologies on the market, and each has its adherents. Each methodology solves the age-old problems of software development in a slightly different way. The core problem is to deliver useful tools to the organization in a timely way.

It is important to pick a standard approach so that you can take advantage of tools and templates that are available to support that approach. If the organization has a standard, the tools and templates are probably already in place and should be able to be adapted to your circumstances.

Standard software development methodologies include training, tools, and templates that would be hard for you to reproduce. You may not want to use every tool or template for every project, but having a well-defined, well-known methodology can give you a leg up on creating a rhythm within the team.

A lot of the new Agile software development techniques are focused around delivering prototypes quickly. The Agile conceptual framework uses iterative cycles within defined time windows to promote the interactions between the end-user and development communities in a structured way. By treating software as an evolutionary process rather than a large, monolithic development waterfall, Agile methods aim to accelerate a software lifecycle process that is sometimes too slow to keep up with the shifting demands of an ever-changing user community.

The pace and the order of operations may be different, but the end goal is always the same. Deliver useful capability to the business in time for the business to be able to take advantage of it.

No two software development situations are the same. An organization needs to develop a rhythm that fits the organization itself, not the organization that spawned the methodology.

From a management point of view, the key is to have a methodology that works in this organization. Pick a methodology that works for your environment and your project. Use ideas that work in your environment, and don't be afraid to apply different rules to different projects if the extra overhead makes sense.

Summary

Managing software teams is both the same as and different from managing other technical teams. A lot of the challenges are the same.

But there are also important differences. Software development is a profoundly creative enterprise. Management's challenge is to unleash the creativity while at the same time steering it in a direction that will maximize business value.

Do not allow your development projects to be hijacked. If the effort is redirected, make sure it is only after a clear-eyed assessment of the benefits and costs of the change, and with buy-in from an established change control process.

Emphasize quality, and measure quality directly with a rigorous testing regime based on a clear understanding of requirements. Use your quality measurements to find ways to improve your team's contribution to your organization's bottom line.

Discussion Questions

1. Describe the development methodology in place in your organization. Describe the ways in which this methodology helps your team add value to the business. How does it hurt your team's efforts? What changes to the methodology might improve your development process?

2. What tools do you use to emphasize the importance of quality? What additional tools can you use?

Further Reading

Berkun, Scott. *Making Things Happen*. Sebastopol, CA: O'Reilly, 2008.

Medinilla, Angel. *Agile Management*. New York, NY: Springer, 2012.

Stellman, Andrew, and Jennifer Greene. *Applied Software Project Management*. Sebastopol, CA: O'Reilly, 2006.

Visualizing Requirements

In Chapter 4, we discussed the importance of identifying requirements. In particular, we discussed use cases and how they can be used to gather and communicate requirements.

Once you have identified a requirement, you need to validate the requirement with the customer. If you find a problem with a requirement definition before implementation, it will save a lot of time and money over finding it later in the development process.

Customers' eyes may glaze over if the requirement is not communicated in a way they can understand. Words are great, but sometimes diagrams are a more effective way to communicate requirements. *Unified Modeling Language* (UML) provides some tools for representing requirements and communicating them between the stakeholder and implementer communities.

We're not going into a full discussion of UML in this book, but some of the tools in UML are so useful that they should be known to every technology manager. There are a lot of nuances in UML that are well beyond the scope of this chapter, but we'll look at some of the main features of these diagrams so that you can interpret diagrams and even draft basic diagrams yourself.

We are also going to discuss data flow diagrams and entity relationship diagrams. These are frequently used side-by-side with the UML diagrams in order to specify functional requirements of databases.

UML Activity Diagrams

Activity diagrams represent workflows. They include methods for representing choice, iteration, and concurrency.

The elements of an activity diagram are

- Activities are represented by rounded rectangles.

- Decisions are represented by diamonds.

- Concurrent activities are represented by horizontal bars marking the beginning and end of the concurrent activities.

- The beginning state is represented by a black circle.

- The end state is represented by a black circle inside another circle.

Activity diagrams may be the most familiar of the UML diagrams. They are similar to the types of flow charts that are used in a lot of different contexts.

In the activity diagram in Figure 13-1, a decision point decides whether Action 1 needs to be run before Action 2. Parallel Action 1 and Parallel Action 2 are then executed concurrently.

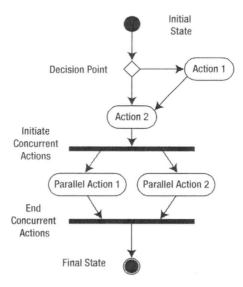

Figure 13-1. Activity diagram

Activity diagrams are useful for describing a step-by-step workflow in an easily readable summary format. This format is particularly suitable for presentations or to provide a discussion framework for working meetings.

Activity diagrams also have the concept of a *swim lane*. This is a large box around a group of activities that are mostly logically separated from other activities.

UML Statechart Diagram

UML statechart diagrams look superficially like activity diagrams. The primary difference is that a statechart diagram tracks system states rather than tracking the order of activities in a workflow. The arrows in a statechart describe the transition.

Statecharts can be useful if the system being described has a limited number of states, and the transitions between those states are known.

Figure 13-2 shows a very basic statechart diagram. The door is either opened or closed, and the transitions are opening and closing the door. There is also a constraint listed, which is that the door can only be opened if it is unlocked.

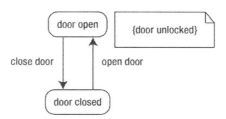

Figure 13-2. UML statechart diagram—door

The statechart diagram in Figure 13-3 shows a more interesting situation. Here the state boxes represent a customer account. The customer submits payment information, and the state of his account reflects that the payment is pending. If the payment is denied, the pending flag is removed. If the payment is accepted, the account is credited.

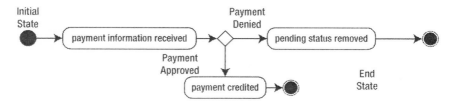

Figure 13-3. UML statechart diagram—payment

Sequence Diagrams

Any nontrivial system features interactions between multiple parts. Usually, these interactions need to take place in a set order. *Sequence diagrams* display information about the order for different object interactions, as well as descriptions of the actions performed between objects.

Each object is represented by a vertical dashed line. The object is designated as "active" when there is a rectangle over the line. Arrows between the objects designate interactions, and the order of those interactions is read from top to bottom.

In Figure 13-4, an end-user calls the help desk, which queries the knowledge base. The help desk then passes the response back to the end-user.

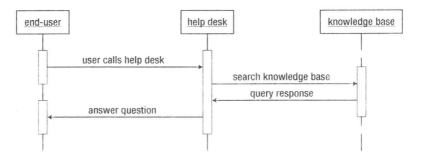

Figure 13-4. Sequence diagram

Note that the "end-user" has a discontinuous active area. This might represent a case in which the user hangs up and the help desk calls back with an answer.

Data Flow Diagrams

A key aspect of any system is how data moves from one component to another. Modeling this data flow is part of communicating how the system works.

Data flow diagrams demonstrate how data flows within a system. Rectangles are actors, circles are data processes, and parallel lines are data sources.

The arrows represent the direction of flow of data within the overall system.

In this case represented in Figure 13-5, the customer requests information from the web/app server by supplying credentials, which are supplied to the data store. Data is returned to the web/app server and then to the customer.

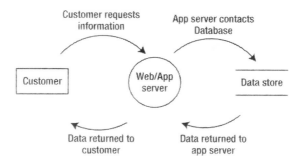

Figure 13-5. Data flow diagram

Entity Relationship Diagram

Entity relationship diagrams (ERDs) are data modeling diagrams. They show the relationship between the data objects in the system.

One of the more common (and useful) ways of portraying ERDs is a format known as a *Crow's Foot diagram*, after the shape of the relationship connector.

Near the end of the connector next to each entity, there is a "0" or "1" on the line. This means "at least 0" or "at least 1." Then each connector is either a straight line or a crow's foot shape, meaning either "one" or "many," respectively.

Figure 13-6 shows examples of several different types of connectors. In this somewhat artificial example, each professor teaches exactly one section of a class. The section is assigned to a room, which may host several sections over the course of the day. Each section contains one or more students, and each student takes one or more class sections.

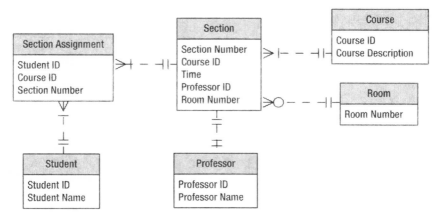

Figure 13-6. Entity relationship diagram

The relationship connector between the table of professors and the table of sections shows a unique one-to-one connection. The one-to-one connection is defined by the "Professor ID" field in the Professor and Section tables.

Similarly, look at the relationship between the Room table and the Section table. The room may be empty, which is why there is a "0" on the Section table end of the connector. Or there may be multiple sections assigned to the room over the course of the day, which is why there is a crow's foot at that end of the connector. The relationship is defined by the "Room Number" field in both tables.

Each class has at least one section, which is why each end of that connector has a "1" next to it. Since a class (say, "History 101") may have more than one section, the section end of the relationship connector shows a crow's foot.

The most interesting relationship is between the Student table and the Section table. That is a many-to-many relationship, since each section may have many students, and each student may take many classes. This is represented by having a "Section Assignment" table representing the section assignments. Each section assignment consists of a course ID, a section number, and a student ID.

(Note that in this model, the student might enroll in more than one section of History 101. Maybe that is okay, maybe it is not. That is exactly the sort of discussion around requirements that needs to be had before the database is created.)

Summary

It is hard enough to communicate and discuss requirements with raw text. Fortunately, there are a number of graphical tools available for portraying requirements.

Discussions of requirements will not get very far if everyone in the meeting has fallen asleep while verbal descriptions scroll across the presentation screen. Pictures can be easier to follow and easier to discuss. Understanding and using standard diagram formats is a powerful tool for any manager to have.

Discussion Questions

1. Think of a simple process in your daily life. Draw a sequence and state diagram to portray that process.

2. Adjust the ERD in Figure 13-6 to allow professors to teach multiple sections.

Further Reading

Braude, Eric J. *Software Engineering: An Object-Oriented Perspective*. Danvers, MA: Wiley, 2001.

Stellman, Andrew, and Jennifer Greene. *Applied Software Project Management*. Sebastopol, CA: O'Reilly, 2006.

Whitten, Jeffrey L., and Lonnie D. Bentley. *Systems Analysis & Design Methods*. New York, NY: McGraw-Hill, 2007.

Integrating Third-Party Software

In some ways, integrating an externally produced software product is more challenging than building a homegrown product. Even if the product is designed specifically for your industry niche, there will be features that you wish that you had, and you also will be paying for features you don't need.

You are going to have to pay software development money to customize and configure the software for your environment. And your organization will need to invest in time and training to reshape its processes to fit the paradigm and limitations of the new software platform.

A good software integration project can save the company huge amounts of money and dramatically improve the company's efficiency and competitive profile. A bad integration project can bleed a company dry. Do everything in your power to make your integration project a success.

Note A package that is intended to fill a core business requirement should not be selected by the technology staff. The decision to seek a solution and the selection of a third-party vendor must be driven by business needs. The evaluation and selection process needs to be owned by a key business stakeholder, and the process must include input from representatives of the directly affected groups.

Research and Vendor Selection

Before you invest in a supplier's product, examine what is in the marketplace. Search the web for review articles about the type of software you are interested in. Then search the web for each of the software vendors mentioned in the review articles.

At each step, look at each vendor's information to see which other vendors they compare themselves to. Then search out those vendors' information too.

During this information search, you will be deluged with information. You need to structure the information you gather, otherwise you will start confusing which vendor has what feature set and what type of reviews. For each vendor, track the following information in your research documents:

- Vendor name and product name.

- Links to the company and product web pages.

- Sales representative and sales engineer contact information.

- Feature set, especially the features relevant to your organization.

- Summarize the sense of the online reviews and comments you find about the software.

- Links to the most relevant or interesting online reviews.

- Pricing information (including maintenance cost information, preferably going out at least five years).

- Information about the frequency of updates and patches.

- Information about the amount of effort required to upgrade or patch the software.

- Training information and links. Are there free online courses? Are training credits offered with the purchase?

- People within your organization who have experience or expertise with the software.

- People in your community (including online contacts) who have information or experience with the software.

- Information about and introductions to vendor user groups. These groups are good forums for learning about new product developments, as well as advocating for new features or fixes to issues.

EVALUATION SCORECARD

As part of the evaluation process, create a *scorecard*. The scorecard should include entries for significant areas such as purchase and maintenance costs, as well as key business and functional requirements.

These requirements should include information security, audit, or compliance requirements.

The software should be considered as a part of your business's ecosystem, existing processes, and culture, and should be scored accordingly.

Each requirement should be weighted according to its importance, as specified by the key stakeholders, and scores should be assigned. This scorecard will be an important part of getting key stakeholders to coalesce around a consensus solution.

A rookie mistake is to assume that you can keep all this information in your head, or that you can easily search the information out on the web as needed. Don't fall into this trap. I can guarantee that there will be some crisis that will emerge when you are in the middle of the search, and when you come back to the search, you will kick yourself for not collecting and organizing your previous search results.

CLOUD-BASED SOLUTIONS

One decision you will need to make is whether your solution will be implemented in-house, or in the cloud.

The *"cloud"* is a generic term describing solutions that are housed by a vendor and accessed over a remote network connection. There are several different varieties of cloud-based solutions:

- **IAAS: Infrastructure As A Service.** This sort of vendor provides a location where virtual servers and storage are available to run the customer's applications.

- **PAAS: Platform As A Service.** Platform vendors typically go one step beyond IAAS vendors. With a PAAS vendor, you will typically get an operating system and program execution environment. Frequently, this will include database, web server, and application layer environments available for running custom-written code.

- **SAAS: Software As A Service:** SAAS vendors typically provide the entire software environment to customers. The advantage is speed to deployment and ease of administration, but vendor lock-in is much more of a concern than it is with IAAS or PAAS.

(Some definitions also include *Network As A Service* (NAAS), which outsources the responsibility for the network connections between different components in the cloud.)

The main advantages of a cloud model are:

- **Cost:** Cloud solutions are typically much cheaper than traditional alternatives.

- **Speed:** It is almost always faster to deploy to a dedicated cloud environment than to build out your own system.

- **Flexibility:** Because the deployment costs are usually lower, there are fewer sunk costs and lower barriers to entry to consider for new upgrades.

- **Easier maintenance:** Maintenance belongs to the cloud vendor, removing an important distraction that you would otherwise have to plan around.

There are some disadvantages to a cloud model as well:

- **Loss of control:** You can have any flavor you want, as long as it is vanilla. Your vendor decides what options to make available.

- **Integration:** Integrating the vendor's software into your environment may be challenging, in part because a lot of vendors' products aren't designed to be interoperable.

- **Lock-in:** Your future becomes tied to the future of your vendor. Especially with SAAS, migrations become difficult.

- **Performance:** Depending on the solution, the performance may or may not be better, but it will certainly depend on the quality of your network connection.

- **Security:** Similarly, the level of security available is determined by what your vendor makes available.

In the end, you have to weigh your options and do what is right for your employer.

Proof of Concept

Research alone will not give you enough information to select a third-party software vendor. If this is a large investment or is a strategic component of your company's business operation, then you will need to go further to ensure that you are making the correct decision.

You can sometimes use the application for a period of time in a "lab"-type setting. This approach is often referred to as a *proof of concept* (**POC**) or a *proof of implementation* (**POI**). You will need to create a short list of vendors based on the research, demos, and the results of reviewing the responses to *requests for information* (**RFI**) and *requests for proposal* (**RFP**).

You will need to plan and work with each vendor to engage in a small but meaningful proof of concept. The goals of the POC should consider all aspects of the vendor package that are relevant to your company, which may include the following:

- Use cases that are important to your business users.

- Validation of all integration points with your technology and applications. The vendor may offer several ways to integrate with your internal applications, so you will want to try to use and compare each method.

- Agreement on how the vendor package will be deployed to your production environment to ensure compliance with your company's release management and deployment process.

- Verification that the package will not conflict with your company's information security or data center policies.

- Specifications for how the vendor package should be monitored, and what tools and mechanisms are available to do troubleshooting.

- Experience using the vendor's customer service and support.

Financial Research

When you select a third-party software vendor, you are making an investment in that company. You will invest significant amounts of money deploying and customizing the software to your organization. Then the people in your organization will spend significant amounts of time adapting their daily workflows and processes to use the software. If the software company or product line disappears, you will have an expensive piece of legacy software that will be difficult to replace.

Investigate the company as if you were going to buy stock in it. Look up financial reports and online analyses of the health of the company. Search the web for information about the company and its place in the competitive marketplace.

Who are the company's main competitors? Is there some likelihood that the company will be acquired? If it is, how likely is your target software package to survive the merger? What are the track records of likely merger partners?

Do the same for the software package. Sometimes companies end up with two or more software packages that play in the same marketplaces. Look into the possibility that your target software package might disappear from the marketplace. If that happens, what would you do for support? Patches? User communities? Consultants and experts?

More than one company has invested in integrating a software package, only to have the software package become an orphan. Do whatever you can to avoid becoming a statistic.

Procurement

Negotiate pricing relentlessly. Point out the features that you don't plan on using, and ask why you should pay for them. And point out the features gap. Ask when that feature will be implemented. Ask what the process is for *requests for enhancement* (RFEs). If possible, get it in writing. And then bargain the price down based on the risk you are taking on the vendor.

Secure proposals from more than one company in the marketplace. Look at the strengths and weaknesses of each proposal. Then discuss these strengths and weaknesses with each of the vendors. Make them sell you their product; part of that is to get the best possible pricing for your company.

The top-line price is not the only cost you should take into account. Take into account the costs of integrating the software, supporting it, updating it, training your staff, and deploying it to your user community.

Frequently you can get credits from the vendor for many of these costs. Look for training credits, or hours from the vendor's consulting arm. Negotiate for years of maintenance bundled in, or at least for not-to-exceed pricing for support at the original discount rate. You will never have as much leverage as you will have prior to signing the deal; you owe it to your employer to extract maximum value. And get everything in writing.

Don't let yourself be swayed by personal attachments to sales reps. Judge the product on the technical merits, including the costs and opportunities at all stages of the product's life cycle.

REVENUE SHARING

Another way to fund the purchase of a vendor package and support is to negotiate a *revenue sharing* arrangement. This is not always an option depending on your business, but it has many benefits. In this scenario, you are offering the vendor to put "skin in the game" in return for sharing in the revenue achieved with a successful implementation and long-term stability and performance of the application.

It is important to make sure that the service level agreement (SLA) includes penalties in which revenue sharing payments are held back for breaches of the SLA. In this arrangement, it is in the vendor's best interest to deliver versions of their application on time and with high quality.

Vendor Management

No matter how friendly the sales reps and sales engineers are, they are in business to take as much of your company's money as possible. Your job is to maximize value for every dollar of your company's money.

Your legal agreement with the vendor should include penalties for failure to perform. Use your leverage to add enforcement language to the agreements with the vendor to deal with nonperformance or failure to meet agreed-on targets.

When there are problems, raise them with your vendor. Be clear. Be definite. Pull out the paperwork and emails, and show them where the vendor has failed to meet its commitments. Negotiate to have the problems fixed, promised features added, and to get compensation for shortcomings in the vendor's deliverables.

You don't have to be a jerk, and you don't have to get angry. In fact, you will be more effective if you keep your temper and stay businesslike. State your case clearly, cogently, and effectively. And demand that the vendor produce the results you thought you were getting when you purchased the software.

Vendor Support

There are several types of support you need from your vendor. At a bare minimum, you need the ability to find out about the product and get help fixing the problems that emerge. Here is a quick list of some types of support you need from your vendor:

- Information on new products and features.
- Methods for communicating problems and enhancement requests to engineering.
- Break-fix support.

- Integration support.

- Links to experts or consultants.

- Access to a user community.

Some vendors spend significant resources developing an ecosystem surrounding a product. These communities of users and vendors can be invaluable in resolving problems, recruiting support staff, and identifying consultants for short-term projects.

Have a phone number of a specific person at the vendor whose job it is to keep your company happy. Then be clear about your expectations and demand excellence.

Integration

Before bringing a software product into the environment, you need a clear understanding of how the product will fit into your environment. What value do you expect to see? What functions will it fill?

Talk to other customers, and verify that the software is capable of what you need. Find out how much effort is required to customize the software for your environment, then estimate the costs associated with that effort. The development costs are part of the project budget for the overall integration, so they have to be included in your proposal to management.

Once you start integration, treat it like any other software development project.

Success starts with your sponsor's buy-in on clear requirement statements. Translate the requirements to clear functional specifications, and develop a test suite to validate the results.

The fundamentals of a software integration project are the same as for a blank-slate development project. Identify the business need, design a way to fill the need, and then execute the design in a timely, professional way.

Deployment

The business needs to own the selection process and be a key part of specifying, procuring, and testing the application during the deployment process. That will help avoid a mentality where there is an expectation will be that a purchased software product will just work. For anything more complicated than an office productivity suite, that expectation is poison.

The conversion from the existing application to the new package needs to anticipate the following:

- What existing data needs to be transferred (and often transformed) to the new platform? This data may come from anywhere in the organization. Some applications calculate data on the fly without storing it in the database. You will need to figure out how this data will be seeded in the new platform since it may not actually be stored in the legacy platform.

- How will users validate that the new platform is correct when the cutover is performed? This is often an afterthought that usually requires the application development team to provide (build) onetime utilities. Typical issues include automating and streamlining validation by the users, frequently by comparing outputs/data between the old and new platforms.

- Any large implementation should plan to include several mock or trial conversions. This is needed to fine tune the detailed steps leading up to the actual conversion/cutover. Understand and optimize the time needed to execute the detailed steps in this process. Remember, you will need to be able to complete the deployment and conversion (usually on a weekend) and have time to do the checkout and fail back in the event the cutover or conversion fails.

- The team needs to start planning early on the approach to be used for implementing the new platform. Will it be a big bang or be done in phases? Will there be a pilot period in which a small set of business groups and users process a subset of the business in production prior to cutting over the rest of the business?

Training

If the stakeholder communities have been intimately involved in the selection, proof of concept, deployment, and testing process, a lot of issues around end-user training will be apparent long before cutover day. Track issues that appear during testing, and keep them in mind for the rollout of the application. The more people you can involve in the POC and testing phases, the less of an issue this will be.

The user-training program is an essential part of a deployment. If people don't use the product because they don't know how, you have wasted your time and your employer's money.

Appropriate training will depend on the nature of the software. It may include documentation with step-by-step instructions and screenshots, it may include presentations, and it may include formal classroom training.

The success of your training program will be measured by your target audience, not your developers. Test your training program on a small group of end-users, and find out whether it was effective. Have them explain the material back to you.

Replacement

Eventually, a software product will need to be replaced. It may be that the package has reached the end of its support life. Sometimes an old package no longer fits in an ecosystem dominated by another product. And sometimes a package has been a complete disappointment.

When it comes time to replace a product, first understand what valuable functions it is fulfilling in the environment. If the proposed replacement products do not share all the required functionality, find ways to fill the gaps.

The entrenched product has the advantage of familiarity, whatever its disadvantages. Your training program will be the key to overcoming this advantage as far as possible. Planning the resources for training is more important in a replacement situation than in a blank-slate situation.

When selecting the replacement, take a clear-eyed look at the strengths and weaknesses of the proposed packages, including the integration costs. You may find that the best alternative is the software package that is already in place.

Summary

Third-party software can be the best way to provide needed functionality to your business. This will only be the case if you can deliver the software, fully integrated, on time, and within budget.

Understand the requirements, both functional and budgetary. Consider the alternatives. Extract maximum value from your vendor. Train your users. Deliver value to your employer.

Discussion Questions

1. Think about a software integration project you have observed. What aspects of the deployment were successful or unsuccessful?

2. Consider someone who is trying to sell software into your organization. What do you need from that sales rep to be successful? What does the sales rep need from your organization?

Managing Outside Your Specialty

There will come a point in your career where you may be asked to manage technical teams who work outside of your technical area. Effectively, you will be a nontechnical manager of a technical team.

This situation poses a whole new range of challenges. You won't be able to rely on your technical expertise to get you out of a pickle. While your technical experience gives you insight into some aspects of your team's work, there are other aspects that will be a mystery to you.

Know What You Don't Know

Technical people are used to being the smartest person in the room. Now you are managing a room of people who know a lot more than you do.

Don't try to fake it. You know how easy it is to spot a poser in your own technical specialty. What makes you think it is harder for someone in a different specialty?

When you speak to your team, you can still pull out your old war stories to demonstrate the importance of the values you are trying to instill in the team. (The time the change went bad to demonstrate the importance of testing, for example.) Technical people are similar enough in mindset that we all appreciate each other's stories.

But when it comes time to discuss approaches to a problem or the guts of a technical issue, your job shifts. You are no longer the senior guy who can propose solutions. Now you are the facilitator to make sure that all the technical experts in the room have a chance to be heard and have their ideas considered.

I had a bit of fun at the expense of nontechnical managers in the Introduction and Chapter 1. When a technical person takes over leadership of a team in a different specialty, that person is effectively a nontechnical manager. Not only that, the new manager has some distinct disadvantages over his or her nontechnical colleagues:

- **Habits of a professional lifetime.** Suddenly, your reflex to just fix what is broken is problematic. Your job is no longer to propose or implement solutions. Your job is to facilitate conversation and to get your team the resources to resolve the problem.

- **Lack of training.** A lot of nontechnical managers have training or degrees specifically about how to manage effectively. Most technical people have focused their attention on technical training, not people management training.

- **Public reputation and persona.** Your nontechnical counterparts are used to dealing with you as the person who knows the answers and can provide solutions at the drop of a hat. If you try to keep this up in a specialty where you don't have the answers, you will just get yourself into trouble.

These are all barriers, but you also bring some significant advantages to the table:

- **Experience managing technical people.** Usually, by the time you manage people in another specialty, you will have been supervising people in your own specialty. A lot of the same skills will translate.

- **Street credibility.** As long as you don't claim to be an expert where you are not, your expertise in another specialty will be viewed with respect by your team. They know that you have paid your dues with late night troubleshooting calls, and that you understand the rhythms and organizational challenges they have to deal with.

- **Credibility with management.** Since they know you have been in the trenches, management will expect you to be able to translate between the technical and nontechnical people in the organization. This may be the most important role of a technical manager at any level.

- **Maturity.** You may not be older than the people you are managing, but you may have a more mature view of how IT works than a lot of your subordinates. (Not all of them, of course. You will rely on the seasoned experts in your team to help you steer clear of pitfalls.)

Listening

Throughout your management career, you have needed to develop skills in listening to your team members. As you have matured, you have recognized that you can't carry the entire load on your own and have come to rely more and more on your team members.

Now *listening* is the skill that will make or break your success in managing your new team. If you try to carry your team based on your own expertise and experience, you will fail. You need the input of your technical people more than ever before.

The advice about integrity and patience in Chapters 1 and 6 now has to be read in a different light. You will need your credibility more than ever. You will only earn it by listening to your team, identifying the roadblocks, and helping shift those obstacles out of the way.

You are not going to learn anything while your mouth is running. Shut your mouth and open your ears.

Demand Clarity

Communication demands two participants. Your job will be to listen. Your staff member's job will be to present the information in a way that you can understand it.

If you don't understand, ask clarifying questions. This doesn't mean that you need to understand every detail of every change request. But you do need to understand some things:

- What is the business impact?
- What are the risks (in business terms)?
- Are we mitigating the risks?
- Have the service owners signed off on the risks?
- Have we done thorough preparation?
- Are the right people involved?
- What obstacles stand in the way?
- What does your staff need from you?

Teach your team members the skill of communicating technical information to a nontechnical audience. It is sometimes painful for technical people to shift gears and "dumb down" a presentation, but it is a necessary professional skill. Your team members need to understand that developing communication skills will help them to be more effective. Nontechnical people are more likely to give your staff the resources they need if the requirements and consequences of the request are communicated clearly.

Process

There are times when your team will be eager to move ahead with a solution before testing is complete. Since this is not your specialty, you will need to ask probing questions before giving the green light to changes.

This is a balancing act. Your team may view this as "interference" in an area where you don't know what you are talking about. Be careful about this dynamic, but you need to start as you mean to continue. Emphasize the importance of planning and testing. If you need to trot out some of your war stories to explain why the process is important, do that. But politely and respectfully insist that the process is followed.

You are no longer in the position of being able to accurately characterize the risks of a change. Over time, you will get a feel for who on the team is a cowboy, and whose judgment you can trust on risk estimates. In the beginning, insist on the process. The process is not just your friend. It is theirs too, even if they don't recognize that yet.

Teamwork

Your team's ability to work together smoothly will be a major predictor of your success. Do what you can to foster a team spirit. This may mean bringing in bagels and beverages from time to time, or it may involve some team playtime.

When you are developing a team spirit, make sure that you keep the focus on the work the team will be executing. It is nice to have a great group of people who like to paintball together on the weekend, but your job and theirs depends on your ability to deliver as a team.

But the ability for people to relax and let their hair down in a trusting environment can sometimes bring deep issues out for discussion. Project meetings can sometimes be so fraught and tense that people don't want to be the messenger who speaks to a serious underlying problem. When people are able to relax and trust, they are more willing to discuss issues in a nonjudgmental, casual atmosphere. And a relaxed atmosphere can also help foster the sort of nonlinear thinking that can point the way to a resolution for an intractable problem.

Blame and Responsibility

Because you really don't quite know what you are talking about, you can be subject to manipulation by team members who are trying to shift the blame for a problem onto someone else.

The best way to avoid falling into this trap is to foster an environment where blame is unimportant. Make sure people are responsible for particular requirements, and that they have agreed to objective criteria for validating those requirements.

But hear out any reservations the person has on accepting responsibility for a particular area. There may be assumptions or interactions that you are not aware of. This is all part of your learning curve as a manager of a new technical area.

Learn

You're a smart person. You have a demonstrated ability to learn technical subjects.

Ask your team members for resources to learn about what they do for a living. They will respect that you are putting in the extra effort to understand what they do.

Don't assume that you will be able to become an expert in something that other people have spent years learning how to do.

As you learn, you will be better able to represent your team's concerns to your own peers and management.

Summary

Managing technical experts in another field is a turning point in your career. It is as big a leap as moving from the trenches to leadership in the first place.

Hold on to the same soft skills that have brought you this far. Don't pose as an expert in a field where you are not. Listen to your technical experts and help them talk themselves to the right answer.

Discussion Questions

1. What is similar between your technical specialty and that of the group you are managing? What is different?

2. Think back to your most effective nontechnical managers. What did they do with your team that was successful? How much of that can you replicate with your new team?

Further Reading

Berkun, Scott. *Making Things Happen*. Sebastopol, CA: O'Reilly, 2008.

Stellman, Andrew, and Jennifer Greene. *Applied Software Project Management*. Sebastopol, CA: O'Reilly, 2006.

Taking Care of Yourself

Work responsibilities can be overwhelming, but you have a responsibility to take care of yourself.

Arranging Time Off

You are responsible for scheduling time off for yourself. In order to take time off, you need to train your team to run without you.

There are some times when you need to be present. In particular, high-stress, politically fraught deployments need you to make the decisions you will have to live with. It is not fair to expect your staff to make a decision in a situation like this. Any decision they make might expose them to criticism from two or three levels above themselves in the hierarchy.

During long projects of this sort, you should be able to schedule time around the rhythm of the overall project. Let people know when you will be away, well in advance. Look for decisions that are going to have to be made, and provide guidance (and cover) to your team beforehand. Enable your team to postpone decisions that people bring up while you are away, and make yourself available by cell phone in the event that people start pressuring them.

Learn to Trust Your Staff

A lot of managers get into the rut of having to be present in order for the team to function. Sometimes this is because the manager does not trust them to execute tasks without direct supervision. More frequently, the manager is unwilling to delegate any decision-making authority to the team members.

If you are in this situation, you need to fix it.

It is possible that your staff is unworthy of trust. In that case, you can train them, or you can release them and hire someone else. (It is very expensive to fire and replace someone, and should not be done without serious consideration.)

Is your staff really unworthy of trust? Or are you being a control freak?

The fact is that other people will make decisions different than the ones you would make, or do things differently than you would. That is okay, as long as the decisions and procedures fall within the clearly defined boundaries you set up for your environment.

The key to managing an effective team is leverage. If you have to be personally involved in every decision, you will be a bottleneck, and your team will be ineffective. It would be better to have your team empowered to make some decisions without you, as long as they are good (but maybe not perfect) decisions.

And if they make bad decisions, you can (calmly) use those cases to teach them a better way to do things. Don't hector them. Don't nag. Explain how you want things done, and provide clear instructions to your staff so that they can make the decisions you would like them to make.

Work–Life Balance

As you empower your team, you need to set reasonable expectations for yourself, and for them. If you drive your team mercilessly with long, inflexible hours, you will have high turnover and will be less effective over the long run.

If you drive yourself mercilessly, you will also be less effective. If you are lying in a hospital bed, your effectiveness is near zero.

Training your team to operate smoothly in your absence and to cover for each other will allow you to all have better balance. Documentation and cross-training are ways to allow everyone on the team to take time off. In a well-documented environment, the on-call person can cover the environment so that people can take time off when they need it.

When you plan schedules, make sure you are making allowances for people to take time off. Part of that may be requesting that your team members get you the information about their expected time off in advance. If they see that it is benefiting them, they will get you the information you need.

Your Physical Health

Take the time and effort to exercise and eat well.

Ours is a sedentary profession. You need to make sure you are developing habits that will keep yourself as healthy as possible. This should include at least 30 minutes of exercise every day, as well as making sure your diet is well balanced.

Some suggestions that have worked for some of your fellow technical people include:

- Take stairs instead of the elevator.

- Schedule your exercise for a particular time of day. If your office is in a walking-friendly location, your lunch break may be a great time to get out of your desk chair and outside for a walk.

- Schedule a particular time for visiting a gym or other exercise location. If you don't schedule it, you won't go.

- Use tracking software to track your diet and exercise. There are quite a few free web sites that will allow you to track your health information. And there are nifty cell phone apps to track the amount of exercise you get over the course of the day.

- Find an exercise buddy who can help keep you motivated on days when you just don't feel up to it.

- Participate in office weight-loss challenges or fitness activities. These can be good team-building activities as well as helping you keep yourself in good shape.

Your mind will only be as good as the engine that fuels it. Make sure to keep your engine in good running order.

Spiritual Health

If your soul needs feeding, you will not be able to lend strength to your team when they need it.

Just to be clear, I am not recommending that you proselytize for your religion in the workplace. That is probably against company policy and may even be illegal. It is certainly unwise and counterproductive.

If you are a member of a church that feeds your soul, that is great for you. But your staff cannot feel like their boss is pressuring them to adopt his or her particular beliefs. If it comes up in casual conversation, mention where your religious community is, and that you feel at home there. Don't go any further than that.

For that matter, spirituality may not have much to do with an organized religion. A lot of people feel that their soul is fed by meditation or study or walking on the beach. If organized religion is not your thing, find something that is.

Career Development

Think about where you want to be in five years. What sorts of experience, education, and expertise do you need to develop to get there? Who can mentor you to get you closer to your goal?

In particular, think about the following things you can do to prepare yourself to go where you want to go:

- **Formal education.** If you never start working on that degree, you are guaranteed never to finish it. Does your employer offer tuition reimbursement? You should be taking advantage of this benefit.

- **Technical courses and certifications.** Is there expertise that you have that is not well-reflected on your resume? If the expertise is important to your career goals, a certification exam can be a good way to bring your expertise out where employers can see it.

- **Job responsibilities.** Work can provide you with a lot of unique experiences. Seek out opportunities to work on project teams where you can learn new, useful skills.

- **Job titles.** Is there a particular title you need to have held as a stepping stone on your development plan? Talk to your boss to see if you can get there internally. If not, you may need to start looking outside your organization.

- **Personal skills and experiences.** Look for volunteer opportunities to pick up skills and experiences that may not be available to you at work.

Discuss your career goals with your manager, and with other people in your industry. They will be able to provide you with pointers and opportunities for development.

Sometimes you have to think outside the box to get the sort of experience you need. Nonprofit organizations frequently need help with technology projects. You can submit proposals to conferences to speak. You can write up and submit magazine and journal articles on subjects that you know well.

Summary

As a manager, your focus should be on your team members. Your concern for their welfare is what will keep them motivated and producing value for your organization.

Part of that is making sure that you are doing what you need to do for your own well-being. Don't be the IT Hero. Be a manager. Manage yourself as well as your team.

Discussion Questions

1. What functions in your team are able to be performed by only one person? What will be the best way to train other people to cover those functions when the primary person is away?

2. What can you do to take better care of your health?

3. Where do you want to be in five years? What concrete steps are you taking to get there?

Further Reading

Harvard Business Essentials. *Manager's Toolkit*. Boston, MA: Harvard Business School Press, 2004.

Watkins, Michael. *The First 90 Days*. Boston, MA: Harvard Business School Press, 2003.

GanttProject

There are many commercial project management packages, such as Microsoft Project. For basic project management functionality, GanttProject is a good free alternative. This chapter gives a quick introduction to the product. As you explore and learn its capabilities, you will quickly grow beyond the scope of this chapter.

Download GanttProject from http://www.ganttproject.biz/download and install it before proceeding. The screenshots and examples in this chapter are based on GanttProject 2.5.4, but most of the information should remain stable across versions.

Main Window

The default Gantt window looks similar to Microsoft Project and has a lot of the same functionality. You can select **Project ➤ New** to create a new project. Right-clicking on the column headers allows you to select different fields to hide or display (Figure A-1). Right-clicking in the work area allows you to add a task. And right-clicking on a task allows you to edit the properties for that task. (Or you can choose **Tasks ➤ New Task** or **Tasks ➤ Task Properties**.)

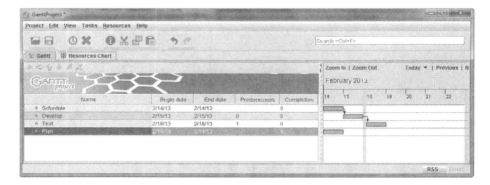

Figure A-1. Basic GanttProject screen

Defining a Project

Project settings can be defined either at the time that the project is created with **Project ➤ New**, or you can choose **Project ➤ Properties** once the Project is open.

The Project Properties dialog box has three sections:

- **Name and description.** This is where you set basic information about the project, such as the **Name**, **Organization**, **Web link**, and **Description** for the project.

- **Calendar.** This is where you would set the **Holiday calendar**, the **Weekend schedule**, and set the **Start date** (Figure A-2).

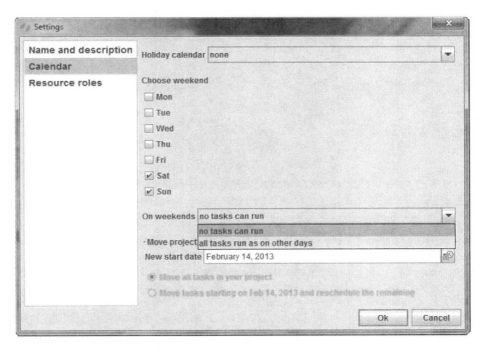

Figure A-2. Project settings: Calendar

- ***Resource roles.*** This is where you can add and delete roles that can be assigned to the resources that will work on your project.

Resources

The **Resources Chart** tab displays the different team members assigned to work on the project. In the example in Figure A-3, you see that it can even tell you when a resource is overcommitted during a given time window.

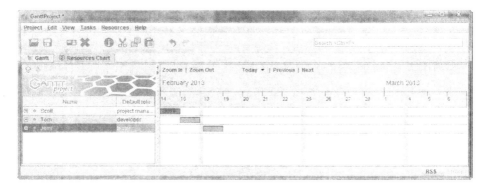

Figure A-3. Resources Chart tab

In the **Resources Chart** tab, you can right-click in the work area to bring up a dialog box to enter information about one of the team members working on the project, or you can use the **Resources** menu (Figure A-4). There are columns to manage holiday time as well as the contact information for each of the people who are working on the project.

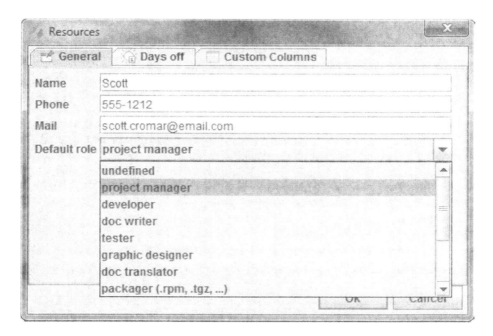

Figure A-4. Resources dialog box

PERT Chart

Similar to other project management tools, GanttProject also allows you to pull up a PERT view (see Appendix B) from the **View** menu (Figure A-5).

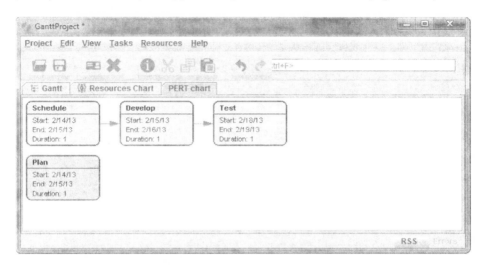

Figure A-5. GanttProject PERT chart view

Summary

GanttProject is a free project management utility that provides the functionality that a lot of managers and project managers need to manage a basic project. It has some quirks, which may be overcome in later versions, but it is relatively stable. It is easy to use and install in a smaller environment or an environment that does not have a standard commercial-grade package.

PERT and Gantt Analysis

Estimating timelines and schedules is one of the hardest things that you will have to do as a manager or project manager. A big part of this is that you will be torn by two conflicting impulses:

- Technical people are optimists by nature. When we think about how long it takes to do something, we imagine how long it will take if everyone leaves us alone, and if everything goes as planned. (Optimism is a wonderful thing, but it is not usually a good projection of what is going to happen.)

- Because we don't want to be the one who delivers something late, we dramatically overestimate how long it will take.

It is good practice to underpromise and overdeliver, but sometimes under-promising leads to a management decision that prevents the company from taking advantage of a new opportunity. Estimates need to be reasonably accurate in order to be useful.

PERT analysis is a discipline that tries to estimate timelines while taking uncertainty into account. A short estimate and a long estimate are used to try to provide an accurate estimate.

Project management software (such as Microsoft Project or GanttProject: see Appendix A) makes it much easier to estimate timelines using PERT and Gantt charts built into the software.

Gantt Charts

Figure B-1 shows a Gantt chart for a simple project. To use a Gantt chart for estimates, you need to have a few elements in place:

- The tasks need to be entered.

- The duration estimates for the tests need to be registered.

- Dependency relationships need to be established.

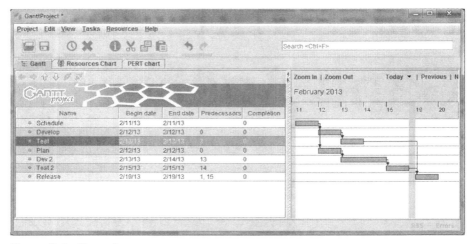

Figure B-1. Gantt chart

Once this information has been entered, the Gantt chart can be examined to identify the critical path.

Remember that the critical path is the shortest possible path through the project. If any of the tasks on the critical path becomes longer, it will increase the amount of time it takes to get through the project. In this case, looking at Figure B-1 and B-2, we see that the critical path is:

Schedule ➤ Plan ➤ Dev 2 ➤ Test 2 ➤ Release

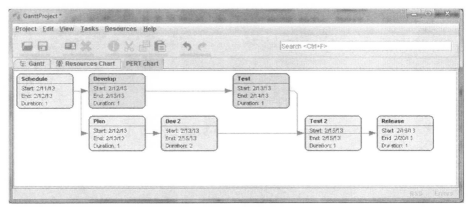

Figure B-2. GanttProject PERT view of a critical path

If any of these tasks takes longer than planned, the release date will slip. In converse, if we can reduce the amount of time spent on these tasks (perhaps by assigning more people to one of the tasks, or finding a way to reschedule it), it may be possible to pull the release date in.

Gantt charts are exactly as useful as the quality of estimates underlying them. If the estimates are reasonably good, they are very helpful to a project manager who is trying to decide which tasks need additional attention in order to keep the project on schedule.

The GanttProject PERT view (see next section) for this project highlights the critical path (Figure B-2). This is useful, especially for a nontrivial project. But the diagram is only as good as the quality of the duration estimates.

PERT Duration Estimates

PERT stands for "Program Evaluation and Review Technique." It represents a methodology for managing the timeline risks in a project.

In PERT, you would measure the duration by getting three different estimates for each task:

- An optimistic, "best-case" estimate.

- A "most-likely" estimate.

- A pessimistic, "worst-case" estimate.

Once you have these three estimates, enter the duration of each task as being:

[(optimistic time) + (4 × most likely time) + (pessimistic time)] / 6.

This weighted average provides a decent time estimate that takes into account the risk that something could go really badly during implementation. People are able to provide three different estimates, and can mentally shift gears to provide each number. This takes some of the pressure off of the technical team, since they can provide estimates based on their experience of what can go wrong while not padding the project schedule so far that the project is abandoned.

But like any other estimation method, garbage in will result in garbage out. Emphasize to the team that they have the responsibility to provide you with their best technical judgment for each of these numbers.

Summary

Gantt and PERT analysis are common tools for providing high-quality duration estimates. Especially when used along with the resource-scheduling features of the project software, they provide a time-efficient way to provide high-quality schedule estimates for a project.

Index

I

A